Reunion Planner

Phyllis A. Hackleman

Reunion Planner

Phyllis A. Hackleman

CLEARFIELD

Reprinted for
Clearfield Company, Inc. by
Genealogical Publishing Co., Inc.
Baltimore, Maryland
1993, 1994, 1995, 1998, 2000, 2005

International Standard Book Number: 0-8063-4559-4

Made in the United States of America

Made in the United States of America.

To my husband, Keith,
for his loving support.

To my friend, John,
for his loving insistence
that I write this book.

TABLE OF CONTENTS

PREFACE

"In a country of such wide extent and room for dispersion as our own, where there are no enduring homes, and no laws tending to their perpetuity, it is not surprising, if we observe among our people in general, a premature hardening of character, the lack of a reverential spirit, and of a delicate sentiment for much which should be esteemed sacred. If our advantages are many; with freedom, range, and opportunities for ambition hitherto unequalled; if the fetters of caste are stricken off, and every one is the maker of his own fortune, there must be, of necessity, from the drift and hurry of our lives, counterbalancing losses. The ties of families are disrupted nearly as soon as formed, while a continual exodus is going on from the older settlements, although abundant lands remain there in a state of nature, as when the Indian roamed over them. From the restricted valleys of New England, the young hurry to the ampler domains of the far West, and from what used to be called the far West, even farther still, over the whole 'boundless Continent,'-- to the / 'continuous woods / Where rolls the Oregon,'-- / to the gold mines of California, at present to the 'Black Hills,' or to any fields of enterprise which promise speedy wealth, never to reassemble around the old hearth-stones. "

My maternal grandmother, Mary Fogle, used to expound, "The more things change, the more they stay the same."

The 1990s find the people of this country still on the move, and for the same reason—opportunities on new horizons.

With the invention of the telephone, telegraph, computer, and now fax machine, we are better able to keep in contact with those dear to us. Even so, we still need to gather "around the old hearth-stones."

INTRODUCTION

"It is safe to say, that many not only lose sight of, but cease to retain any affection for their immediate brethren; that the majority cannot trace back their lineage to the distance of three generations, and are as ignorant of their kin as if they had been cast forth as waifs upon the world, or left as foundlings at some door-way in a basket."

Holding a family reunion sets the stage for bringing people together at regular intervals, allows us to touch the past through shared memories, perpetuates the culture we have inherited from our ancestors, and provides a foundation upon which to build a genealogy.

Hosting a reunion is not an impossible task. It takes only one person to get things moving. I can attest to this from personal experience.

Hosting a reunion need not be complicated. The event doesn't have to be a three-day extravaganza; it can be as simple as a picnic in your backyard or a local park.

My first experience with family reunions was Thanksgiving: the wonderful aroma of turkey and pies; sitting elbow to elbow at the dinner table; playing cards or monopoly till the wee hours.

I'm an Army brat (they call us service brats now). It didn't take long to lose track of aunts, uncles, and cousins. Sometimes we moved four times in a single year.

Friendships blossomed and died quickly. The immediate family was the constant factor in our lives.

My sisters, brother, and I now have families of our own. We live in Ohio, New York, and Pennsylvania. We communicate often by telephone, visit as frequently as possible, and once a year, one of us hosts a family reunion.

When we became involved in genealogy, we suddenly found an expanded family: cousins with the same roots; larger reunions to attend.

In researching my husband's family, I compiled a mailing list of nearly 300 people. Inevitably someone suggested a reunion. It was a giant step from reunions of our immediate family to a national reunion; however, making it happen was easier than I expected and the rewards were tremendous.

I sent out questionnaires and then decided on a time and place. Based on feedback from questionnaires I sent family members, I chose a three-day weekend in Rushville, Indiana. The events would include a Friday night banquet, a Saturday picnic, and lunch on Sunday. Then I contacted the local D.A.R. and the Chamber of Commerce.

About a year before the reunion, my husband and I met his parents in Rushville. Linda Moster, of the local D.A.R., had set up appointments for me with a caterer, the Chamber of Commerce, and the library. She also helped us contact the parks department, a guest speaker, and the minister of the Little Flat Rock Christian Church, which had been founded by the Hackleman family. Then she invited us over for dinner.

By the time I left Rushville, I had arranged for a Friday afternoon Welcoming Reception at the library followed by a banquet with a guest speaker, a Saturday afternoon catered picnic at a pavilion at the county fairgrounds, and Sunday services followed by a luncheon and another guest speaker.

When reunion time arrived a year later, we met my husband's parents, from Illinois, and his aunt and uncle, from California, in Rushville on Thursday. At dinner that evening, we heard a couple who were paying their bill ask if any Hacklemans had been to the restaurant. We immediately piped up, "We're Hacklemans!" Then a couple in the corner said, "So are we." Another group stood and said, "So are we!" The reunion was off and running.

ACKNOWLEDGMENTS

My husband, B. Keith Hackleman, Jr., for original and reproduced photographs.

June Gardner of Tolono, Illinois, for permission to use the photograph of the medallion created in honor of Brig. Gen. P. A. Hackleman.

David and Debra Hackleman of Monmouth, Oregon, for permission to use the photograph of themselves in costume in front the birthplace of Brig. Gen. P. A. Hackleman.

My mother, Della Clem, of Mt. Gilead, Ohio, for permission to use the photograph of her father's family.

My husband's aunt, Idora Alsbury, of Pittsburg, California, for permission to use the photograph of her parents' 50th wedding anniversary celebration.

Introductory paragraphs by F.W. Shelton; Prefatory, Edward N. Shelton; Introduction of Rev. Shelton, and Rev. William Shelton D.D., Discourse, *Reunion of the Descendants of Daniel Shelton at Birmingham, Conn. June 14th 1877*. Newburgh, NY: Ruttenber, 1877.

CHOOSING THE TYPE OF REUNION

"It is surely a proper endeavor, to cherish and keep alive, by such means as we have, the natural, instinctive love of home and kindred; and not only so, but where so much boast is made of widespread intelligence, it were well for us to be neither ignorant of ourselves nor of those we spring from."

This book deals with four basic types of reunions: a backyard picnic, a picnic at a park, a resort weekend, and a three-day weekend at a historic family site.

The information in this book covers a variety of situations. You will want to pick the pieces that fit your occasion and that you feel comfortable with. Remember to start simply and build.

Backyard Picnic

A backyard picnic is one of the simplest reunions to plan. It can accommodate 30 to 40 people. You can have a meal catered, organize a potluck supper, get together for coffee and donuts, or arrange a barbecue.

Your guests will probably be local, traveling less than 100 miles. You may need to provide information about hotels or make arrangements for some guests to stay with local families.

Set aside time to present awards, certificates, or prizes. If time permits, you can include one or two other events such as softball game or a tennis tournament. This type of reunion requires a small budget.

Picnic at a Park

When your reunion grows beyond 30 to 40 people, it's time to move to a public park. Or perhaps someone in your family owns a farm or recreational property. Once you start using public facilities, space is no longer a problem.

Contact the Parks and Recreation Department for information on reserving a shelter. The information operator at City Hall can help you find the telephone number. Depending on the area in which you live, you may need to reserve a site several months in advance. You nearly always have to pay in advance. Prices vary with the location and type of shelter. An open pavilion is less expensive than an enclosed building with restrooms, a fireplace, and kitchen facilities.

If a relative does have a farm you can use, you may want to rent a tent. Rental firms are listed in the Yellow Pages. Tents are available in a variety of sizes; some even have floors in case you want to hold a dance. Some rental firms require a deposit, others payment in full. Be sure to ask who is responsible for setting up the tent, taking it down, and cleaning it. What happens if the tent is damaged?

You will need plenty of tables and chairs. Ask whether they are included in the price of renting a facility. If necessary, you can rent folding chairs and tables from sources like churches and funeral homes.

Hackleman family reunion, Vandalia, Illinois (1920), to celebrate the 50th Wedding Anniversary of Jacob Stucker and Ida May (Jenkins) Hackleman. Original photo courtesy of Idora Alsbury of Pittsburg, California. Reproduction courtesy of B. Keith Hackleman, Jr., photographer.

Fogle family reunion, Kenton, Ohio (c. 1900).
Original photo provided by Della Clem of Mt. Gilead, Ohio. Reproduction courtesy of B. Keith Hackleman, photographer.

Once you have expanded your facilities, you can also expand your program to include a baseball or volleyball game, a dance, craft demonstrations, or any number of other activities.

Be sure to find out if the site you selected has adequate restroom facilities. One bathroom for 100 people can definitely be a problem. Portable units are available for rent.

You will need a more detailed budget to include rental fees.

Resort Weekend

Select a hotel or motel in a resort area with a wide variety of recreational facilities.

Reserve rooms for your group and take advantage of all the hotel has to offer—swimming, tennis, boating, golf, evening entertainment.

Schedule tennis, bowling, or golf tournaments. Charter a boat and take the sunset dinner cruise. Charter a bus and tour a nearby state or National Park, city, or amusement park. Hotels have meeting rooms that they will be happy to rent for your business meeting, welcoming reception, and indoor activities such as a craft demonstration. Hotel caterers can take care of all your meal planning.

Your budget for a resort weekend is a little more complicated. You'll need to determine the cost of the available activities

Hackleman family reunion, Rushville, Indiana (1991). David and Debbie Hackleman of Monmouth, Oregon, at the birth cabin of Brig. Gen. P.A. Hackleman located at Rushville, Indiana. Photo courtesy of David and Debra Hackleman and B. Keith Hackleman, photographer.

and decide whether to include everything in your registration fee or collect money based on individual events.

Weekend at a Historic Family Site

I firmly believe that this is the most interesting and rewarding type of reunion. Walking on ancestral ground creates a special feeling shared by all family members.

Begin by selecting a site significant to your family—an old family home, a church, a cemetery, or an area where several family members settled.

One of the attractions that Rushville, Indiana, offered for the first national Hackleman reunion was an old cabin being preserved by the D.A.R. It is the birthplace of Brigadier General Pleasant Adams Hackleman, the only Indiana general killed in the Civil War. The D.A.R. opened the cabin so that we could wander in and out all afternoon. The cabin is located at the county fairgrounds where we held our picnic and provided an excellent background for group photographs.

Your program for a weekend at a historic site could include tours of an old family home or cemetery. The agenda for Sunday might begin with church services at a church founded by an ancestor or where an ancestor preached. You could plan a banquet or a catered picnic. Present a slide show of important family memorabilia. Ask a family member to prepare a presentation with a specific ancestor as its theme.

For this type of reunion, allow time in your program for genealogical research at local libraries and courthouses.

You should be able to find county historians or members of the local D.A.R. who would be willing to speak to your group about your family's influence on the settling of the area.

Planning will be easier if you choose a hotel to use as a base.

As with a resort weekend, you will need a more detailed budget plan.

VOLUNTEERS

"Many of those brought together saw each other for the first time, and were first made conscious of those ties, which ought never again to be relaxed or completely sundered."

When you decide to host a reunion, you can plan by yourself, recruit a few volunteers, or organize a committee.

There is no reason why you cannot host a small, successful reunion without the aid of volunteers. But as your reunion grows, volunteers—and eventually a committee—will make your job easier. The size of your event will determine the amount of help you need.

These days, everyone is overloaded. No one wants to take on any additional responsibilities. Asking people to assume major tasks will usually lead to disappointment and frustration.

Create a list of all the jobs involved in organizing your reunion. Break it down into as many small jobs as possible. Now, try to match the jobs to people's abilities. If Aunt Louise used to be a den leader, ask her to organize some games for the children. If Uncle Harry is an accountant, ask him to handle the budget. If Cousin Fred owns a print shop, ask him to print address labels.

Children in the family can also be helpful. Young children can stuff envelopes or lick stamps. Older children can help set up tables and chairs or run errands.

People are more apt to help if the task is small and involves something they are good at.

If you are organizing your first reunion and are not familiar with people's abilities, include a list of the jobs in your invitations or promotional letter and ask for volunteers.

As your family reunion grows, you will find that certain people will fit naturally into certain jobs and that you have formed an informal committee.

The next step is to form a family association based on this core group.

A bare-bones committee is made up of a Chair, Secretary, and Treasurer.

As your organization grows, you can add a Program Chair, Registrar, Historian, Event Coordinator, and Publicity Liaison. You may want to appoint a coordinator for each phase of the reunion: accommodations, transportation, certificates, name tags, airport welcoming committee. Each event can have a separate coordinator: welcoming reception, registration, banquets, tours, etc.

As my mother-in-law, Mildred Hackleman, always says, "Many hands make light the work."

SELECTING DATE AND LOCATION

"Few consider--it is a subject in its philosophical aspects altogether too extensive here to discuss, as it concerns the secret mysteries of our being-- how much they are involved in their progenitors."

Selecting a Date

One way to select a date is to plan around a special family event such as a wedding, the arrival of a new baby, or a 25th or 50th wedding anniversary.

Another is to plan in conjunction with an air show, a centennial celebration, or a festival.

Scheduling your reunion around a holiday provides more travel time without cutting into the work week. The drawback is holiday traffic! However, some hotels offer discounts over holidays, especially July 4th.

Selecting a Cancellation Date

You must decide at what point to cancel.

To do that, determine when it will become more expensive to continue than to cancel. Assume no one else will register. Next, add up your non-refundable expenditures to date and the expenditures involved to continue. Then answer this question: Is it worth it to you to go ahead with the reunion?

An increase in the registration fee a month or two before the event to encourage early registration, is discussed in the chapter on budgets (see page 39). The date you pick to increase registration fees should be at least a month before your own cancellation dates with caterers, facilities, and speakers. You also need to leave enough time between this date and your cutoff date for ordering souvenirs. If you haven't received enough registrations by this date, you may be forced to cancel.

If you do decide to cancel, you must send certified letters to caterers, guest speakers, facilities, and any other persons or organizations you engaged for the reunion.

Finally, send letters to all those who registered, and refund monies received.

Selecting a Location

When selecting a location, keep in mind the number of people you expect. Your backyard can probably accommodate at least 30 to 40 people before space becomes a problem. For a larger group, you will need to move to public facilities.

Choosing a local facility will make planning easier. This is not to say a distant location is impossible. I organized a reunion in Rushville, Indiana, from Rochester, New York. I visited Rushville a year before the planned dates and made all the basic arrangements in less than 24 hours. I accomplished the rest with long-distance telephone calls amounting to less than $30.

Where do you start looking for a facility? Start with local hotels or motels, convention centers, party houses. Expand your search to resorts.

Colleges are excellent locations for reunions. They have plenty of sleeping accommodations, meeting rooms, and recreational facilities.

What are some of the things you need to consider when selecting a site?

- What types of accommodations are available? Does the hotel have non-smoking rooms? Does it have handicapped facilities?
- Are shuttles available to the hotel from the airport, train station, or bus station?
- Does the hotel offer off-season rates?
- Are deposits required? How much? When are they due? What is the hotel's cancellation policy? Are deposits refundable?
- Is space available for registration? Does the hotel provide staff to assist with registration? What do they charge for space and personnel?
- Does the hotel have banquet facilities? What percentage is added to meals for tips?
- Are attractions, recreational facilities, golf courses, and shopping located nearby? What hours are they open? Are tours available? If so, what do they cost?

Emergency Information

You will need to know where the nearest hospital and drugstore are located. Does the meeting area use 911? If not, be prepared with telephone numbers for the police, ambulance service, and hospital.

Consider including this information in your registration packets.

TIP: Take along a first-aid kit and an emergency first-aid manual.

Create a Questionnaire

One of the best ways to choose a date and location is to send out a questionnaire. The number of responses can also help you gauge how many people are really interested in attending.

I designed a questionnaire (see page 15) for our Rushville reunion and sent it to everyone on the mailing list—more than 250 people. I compiled the results from the 32 replies and based decisions on the answers below:

- 68% Location of historical significance
- 62% Rushville, Indiana
- 65% August
- 81% Family-style picnic
- Occupational tree
  Slide shows

SAMPLE QUESTIONNAIRE

1. Would you prefer an area that is:
   A. Of historical significance to the Hacklemans?
   B. Geographically centered?
   C. Other. Please specify.

2. If you answered (A) would you prefer:
   A. Easton, PA, near where Michael Hackleman first settled?
   B. Lincolnton, NC, near where the Hacklemans settled?
   C. Abbeville, SC, where Michael Hackleman died?
   D. Rushville, Indiana, where Jacob and his 14 children helped pioneer the territory?
   E. Columbus, MS, where George and his nine children helped pioneer the territory?

3. The earliest year the reunion could be held is probably 1991.
   Would your prefer:
   A. July?
   B August?

4. Would you prefer:
   A. Family-style picnic?
   B. Sit-down dinner?

5. What types of events would make this reunion interesting to you:
   A. Swapping family legends and stories
   B. Displays of Hackleman memorabilia
   C. _____

Now design your own questionnaire. Ask the family where they would like to meet. For example:

- Someone's backyard or farm
- Local, state, or National Park
- Historic family site
- Beach
- Mountains
- Fishing hole
- Hiking trail
- Campsite

Perhaps the family would like to make arrangements through a travel agency. For example:

- Cruise
- Wagon-train excursion
- Steam train ride
- Riverboat rides
- Erie Canal boat tour
- Ecological tour
- Colonial village tour

Choose a location for the purpose of doing genealogical research. For example:

- Salt Lake City
- Washington, DC
- State where family first settled
- Country of origin

TIP: *Your local Chamber of Commerce can provide addresses and telephone numbers of other Chambers of Commerce and convention centers.*

PLANNING GUIDE

"Expressive marks perpetually reappear to occupy their accustomed positions, and so too the self-same smiles which have been worn in ancient times by other faces, beams of pleasant humor and of right good will, as if their primal light were shining yet as bright as ever in the heavens.
The same holds true with respect to qualities of whatever kind, which so often come down to us as an inherited possession, intrenching [sic] themselves in the midst of our individuality, and influencing us as they may."

Absolutely nothing is worse than the sinking feeling that comes when you realize your event is only a few weeks away and you are not ready for it. Avoid the panic that sets in when those months you thought you had to prepare are gone.

You've decided on the type of reunion, the date, and the location. Now it's time to create a planning guide.

9 to 12 months before the reunion:

- Hold a committee meeting
- Create and send out questionnaires
- Choose theme
- Contact Chamber of Commerce, D.A.R.
- Draft preliminary schedule of events
- Reserve facilities
- Contact guest speakers
- Contact caterers
- Set up budget
- Determine cost of registration fee
- Select a cancellation date
- Open checking account
- Start putting together slide show
- Write script for skit
- Reserve period costumes for fashion show
- Send out first promotional letter
- Reserve hotel rooms or compile list of accommodations

- Reserve band
- Reserve transportation
- Hire photographer, videographer
- Compile list of local genealogical research facilities

6 to 7 months before the reunion:

- Send out second promotional letter or follow up on invitations

3 to 4 months before the reunion:

- Order souvenirs
- Order name tags
- Review budget and registrations received, decide if cancellation is necessary
- Assign responsibilities for picnic

6 to 8 weeks before the reunion:

- Notify local newspapers
- Send letter to Mayor
- Send out third promotional letter
- Confirm guest speakers
- Start rehearsals for skit, talent show, or fashion show
- Line up sports equipment
- Confirm method of payment for expenses
- Send reminders to those who haven't registered
- Send reminders to guest speakers
- Touch base with caterers
- Confirm band, photographer, videographer
- Check on picnic assignments
- Purchase decorations
- Purchase picnic supplies

1 to 2 weeks before the reunion:

- Print name tags
- Create sign-up sheets
- Organize registration packages
- Purchase last-minute supplies
- Confirm meal counts with caterers
- Follow up with band, photographer, videographer
- Follow up on picnic assignments

Post reunion:

- Write summaries
- Send thank-you letters to speakers, volunteers, and anyone else responsible for making the reunion a success

CREATING A PROGRAM

"Another advantage was acquired by meeting face to face upon ancestral ground."

Events for your reunion program are limited only by your imagination!

Consider a few things before you decide on a program. Designing a program around a single location provides more time for socializing, requires less travel, and avoids confusion about where to be and when.

Any number of events can be scheduled; however, be sure to pay attention to the needs of your attendees. Grouping too many activities closely together can be exhausting, and leaves no time for socializing or valuable research.

You can run two or more events at a time and offer people a choice.

While designing your program, bear in mind how much help you have and plan accordingly. You don't want to overload yourself to the point that you won't enjoy your own program.

Decide if you want a program theme such as the history of a certain country. Invite speakers to talk about the settlers. Encourage people to come in costume.

Carry the program theme through to your decorations. Make log-cabin centerpieces for the tables. Display actual clothing that belonged to an ancestor.

Decide whether or not you want to provide a program guide. This would include information about the theme, speakers, dates, times, places, events, meetings, officers, and committee members.

No matter what else your program includes, you will want to arrange a head table or podium from which to present awards, certificates, or plaques to family members.

The following suggestions are presented in alphabetical order.

Book Signing

Find out if anyone in your family has written a book. The author may be willing to set aside time to autograph copies.

Business Meeting

You will want to allow time for a business meeting in your program. If you do not have a formal family association, this may be the time to start one. A business meeting gives you an opportunity to discuss future reunions, develop a genealogy, or organize a family newsletter.

If you have a family association, you will want to hear reports from your officers, and discuss current and future projects.

You may want to hold more than one meeting. The committee or officers of the family association may need to met privately before the meeting that is open to the entire membership.

Children's Activities

Books filled with games and crafts for children are available at your local library. Scouting books also provide a wealth of ideas for children's activities.

Church Services

If your reunion is scheduled over a weekend, many people will want to attend church services. See if you can find a church associated with your ancestors. Meet with the pastor to make sure the church can handle extra people.

We included a donation as part of the registration fee and raised a sizable sum for the church. Many people added to the sum during the offering.

The pastor arranged for extra deacons to be present, included a welcoming statement in the program, and offered communion in honor of our presence.

Costumes

Rent or make period costumes and have a fashion show. You don't need a fancy stage or runway. Have people enter from a hallway.

At the Rushville reunion a couple from Oregon rented period costumes and wore them to the afternoon picnic. They had to bring an extra suitcase just for the costumes, but it was well worth the trouble. They were the hit of the afternoon! Everyone else asked, "Why didn't we think of that?"

Crafts

Set up an exhibit area for crafts. Provide materials and arrange demonstrations. Have people make their own name tags.

Dance

Family reunions offer a unique opportunity to pass down traditional dances from the country of origin to the next generation— e.g., an Irish jig, a German polka.

Consider a costume ball. Ask everyone to dress as one of their ancestors would have to attend an old-fashioned barn dance.

Hire a band or deejay, or simply take along a few records and have a dance. Make reservations at a disco or nightclub with a dance floor, or rent a tent with a dance floor.

When hiring a band, get references. If at all possible, go listen to the band yourself. Inquire about deposits, contracts, and cancellation.

D.A.R.

Invite a member of the local D.A.R. to your reunion as your guest. She will be able to answer questions about local research sources. Perhaps someone in your family has written a genealogical or historical book relative to the area and would like to donate a copy to the D.A.R. Make a ceremony of the presentation. Notify the newspaper.

Games

Arrange for a sports tournament—tennis, bowling, or golf. Try a Monopoly, Scrabble, Bridge, Euchre, or checker tournament. Set up a baseball diamond or a volleyball court. Plan a scavenger hunt.

Guest Speakers

A very special feature of the Hackleman reunion special was our guest speakers. This subject is large enough to warrant a chapter of its own; it begins on page 31.

Hayride

Arrange for a driver and a wagon load of hay. This is a good setting for sing-alongs.

Kites

Provide materials to build kites.

Mayor

Notify the mayor about your reunion. With enough advance notice, the mayor's office may send you a letter welcoming your family.

Invite the mayor to participate in a ribbon-cutting ceremony at your hotel to kick off your reunion.

The Mayor of Rushville, Indiana, gave permission for family members to camp at the local fairgrounds.

Meals

See the chapter, *Planning Meals*; it begins on page 56.

Arrange a banquet. It can be a sit-down dinner or a buffet. A buffet seldom costs more and it offers people a choice. If your group includes many senior citizens, you may ask the caterer to limit salt. An angel food cake makes a good dessert for people with cholesterol problems.

A new form of entertainment that is fast becoming popular is the planned banquet. You prepare a menu and ask people to bring specific dishes. Those who cannot cook can bring wine, other beverages, or tableware. You provide the place and do the coordinating. This works very well for small groups.

Mealtime is an excellent time to present awards, make announcements, and share news of births, marriages, and deaths since the last reunion.

Memoirs

At some time during your reunion, be sure to have tables set up for people to display photographs and memorabilia. Ask someone to oversee this table—you don't want anything to be damaged or disappear.

Ask a family member to read excerpts from old letters or diaries. Add to your genealogy by asking someone to research and write about a particular ancestor and then report to the family.

Music

Hire a local group of musicians to play music before or during meals—softly, of course! A harpist is especially nice for this type of occasion.

Quilting Bee

Ask a number of family members each to bring a quilt square and then put the squares together during the reunion. The quilt can be sold, auctioned, or used as a door-prize to raise funds for the family organization.

Reception

You can hold an afternoon or evening reception to kick off your reunion. If you are holding the reception at a hotel, the catering staff will provide you with menu selections. You can also choose between an open bar and a cash bar.

An afternoon reception lends itself to coffee and cookies. For an evening reception, you might have cocktails and hors d'oeuvres.

You may want to operate a hospitality room at your base hotel. Appoint a family member to act as concierge.

```
              AFTERNOON
       WELCOMING RECEPTION

       Refreshment Checklist

  30-cup coffeepot
  Small coffeepot for hot water
  Can of coffee
  Cookies, brownies, and/or donuts
  Hors-d'oeuvres
  Small jar of decaf coffee
  Tea bags
  Cream
  Sugar
  Packets of artificial sweetener
  Hot chocolate
  Soda pop
  Hot cups
  Cold cups
  Napkins
  Small plates
  Spoons
  Paper towels
  Trash bags
```

Slide Show

Put together slides of old family portraits and landmarks to show during your reunion. Genealogists love to share the information they have found.

You'll need a projector, a screen, extra bulbs, and extension cords.

Storytelling

Gather around a campfire and tell stories. A favorite is a continuous story. Have one person start a plot and the next person adds to it. Children love ghost stories!

Talent

Some family members may have a talent to share—playing a musical instrument or singing. Ask if they would be willing to perform for your reunion.

If you are including church services in your program, perhaps the pastor would allow one or more members of your family to perform a song—vocal, instrumental, or both.

Ask a local church if their choir would be available to perform at your reunion.

Tours

Tour the state archives, a museum, the family home, or the city you are meeting in. Arrange for a guided hiking tour.

The Chamber of Commerce will be most happy to provide you with information on available tours near the reunion site. The Chamber of Commerce in your city can also put you in touch with Chambers of Commerce in other cities.

Contact the local chapter of the D.A.R. or the public library to obtain information about local historic sites.

CAUTION: *Tours are usually sold on the basis of a full bus. If only two or three people sign up, you'll need a cancellation policy.*

NATIONAL HACKLEMAN REUNION

Rushville, Indiana

COSTUME   BALL
Admit One

Friday,   August 9, 1991

NATIONAL HACKLEMAN REUNION

Rushville, Indiana

HISTORIC HOUSE TOUR
Admit One

Friday,   August 9, 1991

Video Show

   Take along the videotape from
last year's reunion to show. You'll
need a TV, VCR, and extension cords.

GUEST SPEAKERS

"We think it may be said of all who came, that they derived that kind of inspiration which was to be got from breathing together, like those who pledge themselves from the same cup, their native air, as it flowed from the hill-sides and valleys of Connecticut. It mattered not where they individually happened to be born, the cradling-spot of the family was here, the hearthstone of him from whom all the race descended."

Locating a Speaker

You can find guest speakers for your reunion through the local chapter of the D.A.R., local genealogy clubs, the Chamber of Commerce, and the public library. Another good source for speakers are genealogical magazines.

Nearly all speakers expect a fee. For speakers that do not charge a fee, check with city, county, and state officials; also check with public librarians, archivists, and historians. Another free source for speakers may be a member of your family.

The speaker's fee can be raised by selling tickets, raising the price of the meal to offset the speaker's fee, or including the speaker's fee in the overall cost of registration.

Contacting a Speaker

You may contact the prospective speaker by letter or telephone. If you decide to use the telephone, gather all your facts before you call. You don't want to run up an astronomical long-distance telephone bill, and your potential speaker won't want to wait on the other end of the line while you sort through your notes.

Either way, the speaker will want to know who you are and what organization you represent. Tell the speaker the date, the time, the place, the topic of the speech, and the length of time allowed for the speech.

Be direct about the fee. The last thing you want is an unpleasant surprise in your budget. I recommend a lump-sum payment. If you agree to cover expenses for a speaker be specific about what you will pay for. Otherwise, you may find yourself faced with a bill for a first-class suite, large bar tabs, long-distance telephone calls, first-class airline tickets, or limousine services.

Will the speaker provide equipment necessary for the speech or do you need to provide equipment. Verify exactly what is required. Ask the speaker if handouts are available and whether they are included in the speaker's fee. If not, can the speaker provide you with an advance copy in time for you to have copies made.

Ask the speaker whether tape recording or video recording is allowed.

Finally, establish a cancellation policy in the event you must cancel. Also establish a cancellation policy in the event the speaker must cancel.

Once you reach an agreement, tell the speaker you will send a confirmation letter, and then do it promptly. Be sure to keep a copy for your files.

Preparing for the Speaker's Arrival

Arrange for a member of the family to act as host or hostess for the speaker. If the speaker is from out of town, the host/hostess would be responsible for picking up the speaker at the airport, transporting the speaker to the event, acquainting the speaker with the use of the sound equipment, location of the restrooms, assist in setting up additional equipment the speaker brought, help distribute handouts, and most important of all, confirm the pronunciation of the speaker's name for the introduction.

If you can, provide a microphone and sound system. This is more important than you think. At one reunion, I sat next to a table of small children. Although they were being as quiet as possible, I missed a good deal of the lecture.

Make sure everything is working—lights, projectors, recorders. Is there chalk for the blackboard? Does the speaker need a pointer? Can someone from your group operate equipment, or do union regulations prohibit it?

Position the speaker on a platform if one is available. Everyone wants a clear view. Try to place the platform so that sun coming through the windows doesn't blind the speaker. If this is not possible, pull the blinds or drapes.

If you can, place a clock where the speaker can easily see it. That way the speaker won't have to take off his wristwatch and lay it on the podium or peer conspicuously at his wrist during the program.

Discuss with the caterers when to clear tables. Clattering dishes and wandering waiters are very distracting to both the speaker and the audience. Close the doors to the kitchen if you can.

If you have received permission and are videotaping the speech, turn off any overhead fans. Every time the speaker pauses for a breath, the video recorder tries to equalize the sound volume in the room, resulting in a roar on the sound tract.

Finally, after you have introduced the speaker, sit down in the audience. Let attention focus on the speaker.

Cancellation

Forewarned is forearmed, so be prepared for the speaker to cancel. What will you do if your speaker suddenly needs an emergency operation and the substitute the speaker usually sends is in Europe?

Ruth Metzler, President of the Rochester Genealogy Society, handled the situation quite effectively by having in reserve a slide show she had put together years before. She enhanced her presentation by reading old letters from one of her ancestors.

The point is, be prepared for disaster!

SAMPLE CONFIRMATION LETTER

Dear Speaker:

This is to confirm our conversation of this morning, January 24, 1990. It is my understanding that you will speak at the Hackleman Family Reunion on August 9, 1991, at 7:30 pm. at Winkerby's Restaurant, 205 N. Main Street, Rushville, Indiana.

We are looking forward to hearing how the Hackleman family helped influence the settling of Rush County, Indiana.

I understand you live nearby, and will not need a hotel reservation, and that you will provide your own transportation.

I will meet you at the restaurant at 5:45 p.m. to acquaint you with the sound system.

If you need any special equipment, such as a blackboard or slide projector, please let us know as soon as possible so that arrangements can be made.

As we discussed on the phone, we would like a 30-minute talk followed by a 10-minute question-and-answer period.

Would you please send me biographical material for my introduction? We would also appreciate two black-and-white glossy photographs. The local newspaper has agreed to print a photo layout. We would like to include a photo and the biographical material in our promotional letter.

We agree that your fee will be $250 and that no travel expenses are necessary. You and your spouse are cordially invited to join us for dinner at our expense. Dinner begins at 6:00 p.m.

We are delighted that you will be able to speak at our reunion and are looking forward to meeting you.

Sincerely,

CREATING A BUDGET

"One of our strongest regards is for our home and our ancestors. It is not that our home is more valuable than others; for the poorest hovel has a rich and glowing charm, to those who were born and bred in it, which the richest and most attractive palace cannot give, and ancestors are associated with much that is most dear in life."

The more complex your reunion is, the more complex your budget becomes.

For a backyard picnic, you need to purchase food and beverages. You may need ice, charcoal, decorations, party favors, invitations, and stamps. You can absorb the cost yourself, ask people to provide specific items, or charge a nominal registration fee.

For a picnic in the park, additional expenses include renting a building or pavilion and possibly some promotion or advertising. Now you'll need a little capital to work with.

For a resort weekend or a three-day event at a historic family site where everyone pays for their own hotel rooms and meals, your additional expenses may include long-distance phone calls, events such as tours, and speakers. You will need to make deposits, pay telephone bills, and purchase printing, postage, and office supplies.

Since your budget determines the registration fee, do your best to keep costs down.

Here are some additional items you may want to include in your budget:

- Certificates, awards, and prizes
- Handout materials
- Donations to a specific group (church, D.A.R., library, scholarship fund)
- Souvenirs
- Sales tax
- Tips
- Equipment rentals
- Advertising
- Door-prizes
- Name tags
- Meals and beverages included in the registration fee
- Entertainment
- Expenses for guest speaker
- Photographer/videographer
- Decorations
- Promotion materials
- Meeting rooms
- Signs

If this is your first reunion, add 5- to 10-percent to your registration fee to cover those "unexpected expenses." You can always use any excess funds as seed money for the next reunion, donate it to a worthy organization, put it toward a scholarship fund, or use it to print a family history.

Checking Account

Open a separate checking account for all reunion transactions. It is all too easy to confuse personal and reunion funds in one account.

Keep Records

To help plan the next reunion, keep a record of your expenses.

Paying the Bills

Check with all persons and organizations on the required method of bill payment. Some will want full payment well in advance; some may require only a deposit with payment in full immediately before or after the event.

Find out if personal checks are acceptable. If not, how must you pay?

Out-of-Pocket Expenses

If you are working with a committee, establish a clear policy on reimbursement for out-of-pocket expenses. If out-of-pocket expenses are to be reimbursed, make sure everyone saves all receipts for the treasurer.

If your expenses exceed your income, don't despair. Here are a couple of alternatives to swallowing the expense yourself:

Provide a financial statement to the family members, tell them you underestimated the expenses, and ask for a donation. Buy an expensive bottle of wine or champagne, a box of good candy, or some other item and hold an auction. Tell family in advance *why* you are holding the auction.

Cancellation and Refund Policy

Your invitation or promotional letters need to state your cancellation policy clearly. Clearly explain how you will notify people in the event the reunion must be canceled, as well as when and how monies will be refunded.

Establish a refund policy before collecting any money. Set a date beyond which no refunds will be made. State the policy and date clearly on the registration form.

Increased Registration Fee

Establish a date beyond which the registration fee will be increased; this will encourage people to register early. The increase must be at least $5 for anyone to take it seriously. Check your event calendar. How soon do you have to cancel the caterers, the facilities, and the speaker? Set you date at least one month prior to this time.

Budget Planning

The budget is the most vital part of the planning process. If registration is too high, people won't come. If it's too low, you end up paying bills out of your own pocket.

Here's a bit of advice to help you plan: If you have 250 addresses on your mailing list, you can expect an attendance of 50 to 60 people including spouses and children. You should plan your budget based on the smallest expected attendance. Any monies left over can be donated to the family association, to the preservation of a historical place associated with the family, to the establishment of a college scholarship, or to any number of other causes.

First, determine the costs that are the same for every person, such as meals and a donation for a specific purpose. These are your variable costs. Add in allowances for price increases, tax, and gratuities. Try to get your caterers to guarantee prices. If they won't guarantee the current prices, at least find out how much of an increase to expect and adjust your budget accordingly. Find out if there is a price break for larger parties.

Sometimes you can actually save by ordering more meals than you need to get a lower overall price per person. For example: Your per-person price for fewer than 50 people is $10.00; your per-person price for more than 50 people is $8.00; 45 people have registered.

    45 x $10.00 = $ 450.00
    50 x $ 8.00 = $ 400.00

By ordering an extra five meals, you save $50.00. If it bothers you to order five meals no one will eat, invite five guests.

Second, and more difficult to estimate, are your fixed costs. Some of these may be souvenirs, rental fees for facilities, meals for speakers and other guests, telephone bills, postage, copies, offset printing, door-prizes, decorations, and office supplies. When you first make up a budget, you will have to estimate these costs.

Add the total estimated fixed costs and divide by the lowest number of people expected to attend. This gives you the administration fee you need to add to the variable fee, which in turn gives you your ideal registration fee.

The following formulas will help you figure your registration fee. (Admin. = administration.)

Fixed cost ÷ Lowest # of people = Admin. fee

Admin. fee + Variable cost = Registration fee

Create a best-case scenario by listing every expense you can think of. Assign high estimates to each item.

Next, create a partial-case scenario, in which you absorb some of the costs yourself, reduce the number of expensive awards, and decide to use only one color on the logo design for the souvenirs.

Finally, create a worst-case scenario. What can you really do without? What are you willing to pay for out of your own pocket if necessary? What can you get donated?

Take a closer look at variable costs. For example, are children's meals cheaper? The caterers I worked with on the Hackleman reunion charged half price for children aged 4 to 7, no charge for children 0 to 3.

Do you plan to give children souvenirs? We decided not to give souvenirs to children under 18, and were able to come up with a graduated registration fee.

VARIABLE COSTS*

| | Fewer than 50 | | More than 50 | |
	Adult	Child	Adult	Child
Fri. Buffet	$10	$5	$8	$4
Sat Picnic	8	4	7	4
Sun. Lunch	10	5	6	3
Donation	2	0	2	0
Totals:	$30	$14	$23	$11

*All numbers rounded up to nearest dollar.

Use the "Fewer than 50" numbers for your budget. If more than 50 people register, then you will have extra money for something else such as decorations or an extra guest speaker.

FIXED COSTS*

	BEST	PARTIAL	WORST
Souvenirs	800	700	125
Facilities	100	100	100
Awards	150	100	25
Office Supplies	60	30	0
Telephone	45	25	0
Promotion	500	500	430
Speakers	200	100	0
TOTALS	$1855	$1555	$680
÷ Lowest # people	50	50	50
= Admin. fee	$ 38	$ 32	$ 11
+ Variable cost per Adult	$ 30	$ 30	$ 30
= Registration fee per adult	$ 68	$ 62	$ 41

*All numbers rounded up to nearest dollar.

Now you must decide whether a $44 registration fee will bring in more people. Will a $68 registration fee keep people from coming? Do you need to try some cost-saving methods? Here are some suggestions:

- By reducing the artwork to a single color, you reduce the price of your souvenirs by $80.

- Buy and decorate T-shirts instead of ordering professionally made souvenirs.

- Eliminate the fancy plaque and trophies and give out certificates to reduce the cost of awards.

- Reduce the cost of office supplies and long-distance telephone calls by absorbing all or part of the cost yourself.

- Be more discriminating about your mailing list.

- Reduce or eliminate the number of paid speakers.

MANAGING INFORMATION

"Avoiding extremes, and looking at the matter in a sensible way, it is of great practical utility that the records and statistics of families, however humble, should be preserved inviolate. They are of interest, or should be, to those whom they concern, as they are not infrequently of inestimable value. There is a kind of information which begins to be appreciated, when the 'gain thereof' is that of houses and lands, dollars and cents. We are, however, somewhat apt to sneer at those who grope for dates among dusty depositories, or give themselves to the driest compilations. But well-authenticated dates often clear up more important matters than those which they adhere to."

Whatever method you choose to manage your budget and other information (computer software, index cards, or handwritten ledger sheets), you will need to organize the following information:

- Name of each person attending
- Address of each family
- Telephone number in case of emergency
- Amount paid
- Amount collected toward each meal
- Amount collected toward each event
- Amount collected toward administrative costs

You will also have to track how many extra meals to order for your speakers and guests.

Mailing List

The first thing you need to do in managing information is create a mailing list. If you have access to a computer with software for making labels, great. If not, old-fashioned index cards are more work, but get the job done.

Ultimately, someone will suggest obtaining a bulk mail permit from the post office. I don't recommend it. The permit is costly to obtain and costly to maintain. Furthermore, bulk mail receives the last priority and can take three to four weeks to deliver. More than once, I have received invitations to conferences and reunions after the event was over—thanks to bulk mail!

First-class mail is faster and is forwarded up to six months after someone has moved. I invested in a rubber stamp that reads "Forwarding & Address Correction Requested." When this statement is on an envelope, the post office will forward after the six month period and will send you a notice with the new address. This service costs you the price of a first-class stamp.

My mailing list for the Hackleman family contains more than 400 addresses. I hand-addressed envelopes—once. Then I bought a data management program for my computer. Once started, a mailing list can grow to more than 3,000 names. So when you set up a system, keep an eye toward the future—mailing lists, once started, have a way of expanding.

You can add to your mailing list in several ways:

- Ask the family members you correspond with to send addresses for the family members they correspond with.
- *CompuServe Information Service*, P.O. Box 20212, Columbus, OH 43220, has a data base of more than 80 million names, addresses, and phone numbers. They do charge a fee.
- Major libraries have telephone books for

many cities. Telephone books can also be ordered from your local telephone company for a fee.
- Advertise in *Genealogy Helper*, *Heritage Quest*, or *Ancestor* magazine.

Once you have compiled the list, you need to be maintain it. People move-frequently!

Create a method to track those addresses that are ACTIVE and those that are INACTIVE. When a new address comes in, check it against your file. Is it really new or just a recirculated old address?

TIP: Back up your computer files or give someone a copy of your index cards for safekeeping.

As Your Reunion Grows

As your reunion grows, you may want to keep track of other information such as volunteers and their talents, services available, hotels, and companies or people willing to make donations.

Registration Form

Your registration form should include the following information:

- Registration fees (graduated price list if applicable)
- Date that registration fees increase
- Deadline for registration
- Late charges
- Cost of extra souvenirs
- Cancellation information

- Refund policy
- Place for name and address
- Place to list other persons attending (for name tags)
- Name and address of registration chairperson
- Checks payable to: _____
- THIS FORM MAY BE DUPLICATED

Inevitably someone will want to register for just one day of the reunion. Someone else will want to "just buy meals." You must decide ahead of time if you can make these exceptions and handle the extra bookkeeping involved.

You should be prepared for walk-in registrants. These are the people who decide the night before the reunion that since they have nothing else to do, why not drop in.

You will also get calls the week before the reunion asking if it's too late to register. If you do not have money in hand, be careful about including these people in the meal count; they may or may not show up. I made that mistake, and it cost me ninety-six dollars out of my own pocket. Please consider yourself forewarned! Keep in mind that 5- to 10-percent overage that the caterers normally prepare.

Confirmation Letter

Every person who registers should get a confirmation letter. Verify the number of people per family registering, the names, the check number and the amount, and any extra souvenirs ordered.

At first I tried to write personal letters to each person who registered. This became quite cumbersome and I finally resorted to a form letter—not as personal, but much more efficient.

With the confirmation letter, I suggest you include hotel and campground information, library and courthouse information, a map showing how to get to the Welcoming Reception and/or Registration, an updated schedule, and your latest count of people registered and the states they represent.

If you are trying to build a genealogy, send forms requesting genealogical information.

Update Letter

It never hurts to send out a letter about two to three weeks before the reunion with the final schedule, any last-minute changes, the latest count of people attending, reminders to bring displays, reminders to bring door-prizes, directions, special instructions, parking information, and a Checklist for Attendees.

SAMPLE CONFIRMATION LETTER

Phyllis A. Hackleman
25 Lake View Terrace, Rochester, NY 14613-1710
(716) 458-0386

May 10, 1991

Henry Hackleman
24 Terrace View Lane
Anytown, NY 14000

RE: Hackleman Reunion, August 9, 10, 11, 1991

Dear Henry,

This is to confirm receipt of your check # _____ in the amount of $_____.00 for:

_____ Adults age 18 and over
_____ Child, age 8 to 17
_____ Child, age 4 to 7
_____ Child, age 0 to 3
_____ Extra Coffee Mugs

In addition to the hotel information, I am enclosing some information on local libraries and a map that will assist you in finding the Rushville Public Library on Friday. The Rush County Chamber of Commerce is providing us with detailed county maps, which will be available on arrival.

Looking forward to meeting you in August.

Sincerely,

Phyllis A. Hackleman

SAMPLE LIBRARY LIST

The following are some of the libraries
you may want to visit while in Indiana:

Indiana State Library
140 N. Senate Avenue
Indianapolis, IN 46204
(317) 232-3675

During the months of June, July, and
August, the genealogy department is open
M-F 8:00 a.m. to 4:30 p.m.

Allen County Public Library
900 Webster Street
Fort Wayne, IN 46802
(219) 424-7241

Their genealogy department is open
M-Th from 9:00 a.m. to 9:00 p.m.
Fri. and Sat. 9:00 a.m. to 6:00 p.m.

The Allen County Public Library is home
to one of the finest genealogical
collections in the country.

Wabash County Historical Museum and
Memorial Hall
89 West Hill Street
Wabash, IN 46992
(219) 563-0661
Hours: M-F 9:00 a.m. to noon

This organization is home to Elijah
Hackleman's diaries and scrapbooks.

CHECKLIST FOR ATTENDEES

- Old family photographs
- Memorabilia
- Confirmation letter
- Sense of humor
- Camera:
    extra batteries
    lots of film
    plenty of videotape
- Tape recorder:
    fresh batteries
    extra cassettes
- Willingness to help
- Comfortable clothes and hoes
- Enthusiasm
- Pencils, pens, and paper for
    taking research notes

RESERVING FACILITIES

"Suffice it to add, that the charming hospitalities of our host were in accordance with the sentiments which prompted them, and the hours were winged with gladness, as his kinsmen-guests clustered around his board, or rambled in couples, or in companies, over his beautiful grounds, which, situated on an elevated part of the thriving town, overlooked an expanse of meadows in the flush of summer bloom, with a glimpse of the Housatonic River in the distance."

The person in charge of facilities and physical arrangements is usually the committee chair. Included in this assignment is finding and renting facilities, making sure speakers and musicians have the equipment they need, making sure sufficient restrooms are available and accessible!

A large reunion may require reserving a banquet hall or even a convention center. Meet with representatives. Go over contracts carefully. Spending the money to check with a lawyer may save you money later.

Many hotels, party houses, banquet halls, and convention centers raise their rates during some seasons and lower them during others. Holidays and the weather are a couple of the determining factors.

Some restaurants, churches, town halls, and colleges also have facilities available for rent.

Do a little comparison shopping. Put on your best "What kind of deal can I get on that car?" face and see what you can negotiate.

Ask about off-season rates. Even if the place you want doesn't have regular off-season rates, they may be willing to negotiate price or throw in some extras to get your business such as free lodging for the organizer, a free meeting room, or a free hospitality room.

When renting facilities, ask if a stage is available for your talent show, fashion show, or skit. Is there a charge for using it?

Ask if you are allowed to decorate or hang signs on the walls. Rules vary with the facility.

Find out what type of sound equipment is available or if you have to supply your own. How much is it going to cost? Do regulations prohibit your providing your own equipment? Will union regulations keep you from operating equipment yourself?

Is a podium available?

A convention center will rent any or all of their available space. They will also rent you just about anything else you need: sound equipment, video equipment, podiums, viewing screens, flip-chart stands, TVs and VCRs, decorations, and a long list of other items. They will contract for flowers and balloons. They have caterers ready to help you plan meals and coffee breaks. They may also insist on an insurance policy.

Here are the important questions to ask when renting facilities:

- Are restrooms adequate? You need more than one restroom for 200 to 300 people. Can portable units be rented?
- If you are having a picnic, who is responsible for setting up and tearing down tables and chairs?
- What are the policies regarding alcoholic beverages?
- Do you need liability insurance?
- Is a cleaning deposit required? Arrange an inspection tour to avoid questions later.
- What do you do with trash?
- What time can you get in to set up?
- Who has the key and where do you return it?
- Can you hang anything on the wall? How? Can you use tacks, tape, or plastic adhesive?
- Is the facility accessible to wheelchairs?
- Is a kitchen available for making coffee? Who is responsible for cleaning?
- What is the seating capacity?
- What is the smoking policy?
- Is sufficient parking available? What about handicapped parking?
- Will the facility write a Letter of Agreement or do you need to do it yourself?

PLANNING MEALS

"It is not, however, within the scope of this preface to refer to all the many pleasing incidents of a reunion, which will shed its hallowed influence over a life-time, or of a social converse which, it is to be hoped, will ripen into better acquaintance and enduring friendships."

One planned meal per day gives everyone time to be together and puts less strain on the organizing committee. It also keeps registration fees lower.

Someone in nearly every group will want a choice of entrees. There are two problems with this decision: some people will forget what they ordered, and some will change their minds. If you must offer a choice, use place cards with each person's name and chosen entree.

Planning a buffet is much easier. A three-meat buffet should be enough to guarantee something for everyone.

Tickets

You must decide whether or not to require tickets for meals. If you use tickets, select a different color for each meal. If yours is the only group in the building, name tags may be sufficient.

If you are planning a sit-down dinner with a choice of entrees, tickets provide an advantage. You can write the entree choice and the person's name on the ticket. It's amazing how many people don't remember what they ordered!

Seating

For a large affair, you may want to number the tickets and assign tables as well. Seating a hundred people can be difficult without assigned seats. Inevitably, a family of five arriving at the last minute will find their five empty chairs at five different tables!

Potluck

Potluck suppers where everyone brings a dish to pass also require planning to avoid a table of nothing but macaroni and cheese. For a group of six families, four families should provide a meat dish for six people; one family should provide potatoes for twenty-four people; and one family should provide vegetables for twenty-four people. This formula was worked out through years of experience with Blue and Gold dinners while our sons were in Cub Scouts.

You can plan a potluck picnic in several ways. Each family can be responsible for all their own food, beverages, and table service. You can ask each family to bring their own meat, beverages, and table service, as well as a dish to pass. If you include a small charge in the registration fee, the committee can purchase beverages and table service. You can include the cost of the entire meal in the registration fee, and have the committee purchase everything. Finally, you can do the cooking yourself or consider having your picnic catered. When people are traveling long distances, it is difficult to prepare food for a picnic.

Some families will have to travel to

attend your reunion. These people will find it difficult to cook food ahead of time. Perhaps these families could supply items such as paper goods, charcoal, ice, beverages, condiments, or decorations.

Whatever you decide, spell it out in your invitations.

The following is a checklist of the items you may need for a picnic.

- Tables
- Chairs
- Grills
- Potholders
- Matches
- Charcoal and lighter fluid
- Serving utensils
- Paper towels
- Coolers, ice chests, or garbage cans for icing down drinks
- Ice
- Soda, Iced Tea
- Beer
- Coffee urns, coffee (regular and decaf), sugar and artificial sweeteners, cream or powered cream, teabags, hot chocolate
- Can opener
- Condiments
- Sharp knives
- Cutting board
- Foil
- First-aid kit
- Insect repellent
- Detergent, scouring pads, sponges, dish rags, dish drainers
- Trash bags
- Tent
- Portable toilets

For groups of more than 20 to 30 people, portable toilets can be rented for that picnic on a family member's farm.

Tents and pavilions can be rented. Some come with dance floors. Check with a church group or a funeral home for chairs.

If a cleaning deposit is required to rent a pavilion or hall, arrange a pre-site inspection and a post-site inspection. Be sure you know exactly what is required to get your deposit back.

Picnic Setup

Set your tables up so that people can reach the food from both sides.

Create different areas of operation. Separate alcoholic and nonalcoholic beverages. Place desserts away from the other food tables to avoid congestion. The cleanup area should be away from the food tables.

Think recyclable! Put out separate containers for trash and recyclable.

TIP: Give yourself a break. Assign people to cook, serve, setup, and cleanup. You deserve to have a good time too!

Caterers and Restaurants

The local Chamber of Commerce will have a list of caterers you can contact. Ask the caterers to send you sample menus and prices.

Check with local church groups. Many will be happy to arrange meals to raise money for the church.

Once you have a list of caterers and restaurants, ask your friends and neighbors for references. Go to a restaurant and sample the food—before contacting the management. Was the food good? How was the service? What about the acoustics for the guest speaker?

Do a little comparison shopping. Give each caterer or restaurant the same information so that you can make accurate comparisons.

Here's a list of the questions to ask the caterer or restaurant:

- How many people can the restaurant seat?
- Is there is a price break for larger parties?
- Do you need to guarantee a minimum number of meals? How many?
- Does the price include sales tax and gratuities?
- Does the price include any overtime the kitchen staff might incur?
- Are there any penalties for canceling?
- Are decorations provided? At what cost? Can you supply your own? What's allowed? When can you put them up? Take them down?
- Can you bring your own alcohol? Who will supply the glasses and corkscrew? Can you use the restaurant's refrigerator to cool wine or champagne, or do you need to bring an ice chest?
- Are restroom facilities sufficient?
- Is parking adequate? Handicapped parking?

- What about a stage, sound equipment, or podium for your entertainment needs?
- What is the policy on smoking? Most party facilities allow smoking unless you specify otherwise.

Here's the information the caterer or restaurant needs from you:

- Date
- Time
- Number of adults
- Number of children
- Number of high chairs needed
- Type of menu you want—sit-down or buffet, number of entrees, meats for the buffet
- Type of beverages
- Dietary restrictions
- When to serve and when to clear tables (Can they clear before the guest speaker to eliminate clatter during the talk?)

When working with a caterer or restaurant, be sure to book well in advance. Most of the popular places may be booked as far as a year in advance.

Caterers usually prepare 5- to 10-percent more meals than you guarantee. Take this into consideration when preparing your final meal count. Once you give the caterer your final meal count, you pay for the meals whether or not someone eats them!

I learned a costly lesson with a reunion that included a Sunday lunch. Nearly a third of the group left immediately after church. I paid for 24 meals that no one ate. It was a little less painful knowing the money went to a church, but still—ouch!

I strongly recommend that you create a checklist for meals and send it to attendees. Ask them to check off which meals they will be attending. The checklist should clearly state that meals will not be ordered unless attendees return the list. This can save you a lot of money if people leave early.

Finally, keep in touch. Reservations are made months in advance. Check with the caterer or restaurant a couple of months before the reunion with your estimate of the meals needed. You will need to contact them the week before to give a final count of meals and confirm any other arrangements you made.

Sit-Down or Buffet?

My personal favorite is the buffet. It offers a larger selection of foods and is more likely to have something to suit everyone, including the children.

```
┌─────────────────────────────────┐
│        SAMPLE BUFFET MENU        │
│                                  │
│                                  │
│            Roast Beef            │
│               Ham                │
│          Fried Chicken           │
│       Selection of Salads        │
│             Potatoes             │
│              Rolls               │
│       Variety of Desserts        │
│       Lemonade or Iced Tea       │
└─────────────────────────────────┘
```

SAMPLE CHECKLIST FOR MEALS

Help us plan our meal count. Please
check the meals your family plans to
attend.

_____   Friday banquet

_____   Saturday picnic

_____   Sunday lunch

Please return immediately. <u>Meals
will not be ordered unless you return
this checklist.</u>

Thank you

```
NATIONAL HACKLEMAN REUNION

       Rushville, Indiana

          DINNER TICKET
       1 Adult age 8 or over

        Entree:  Chicken

     Friday,  August 9, 1991
```

```
NATIONAL HACKLEMAN REUNION

       Rushville, Indiana

          DINNER TICKET
       1 Child age 4 to 7

       Entree:  Roast Beef

     Friday,  August 9, 1991
```

Consider using different-colored tickets for each meal. You may even want to use different colors to help distinguish between an adults' and children's tickets or different entrees.

ACCOMMODATIONS AND TRANSPORTATION

"The consolidation of States is secured by the cementing not only of atoms, but of masses, and the harmony of States, by that of happy and undivided families."

Central Hotel/Motel

One of the early decisions you need to make is whether to hold your all your events at a hotel/motel or to use another facility and let folks make their own hotel/motel choices.

Holding all your events at a hotel/motel offers several advantages. A centralized location eliminates hectic running around and the need to arrange for mass transportation. It also puts all your guests under one roof, which makes visiting much easier.

There are also some advantages to holding your event in a small town where hotel/motel rooms are limited and your guests are scattered to the four winds. Speaking for myself and many genealogical friends, we have to go to small towns to locate our ancestors. Small towns have a friendly atmosphere and prices are usually quite reasonable.

Negotiation

Once you have decided on a location, be it a central one or a scattered one, and a tentative program, it's time to do a little comparison shopping and a little negotiating.

First, put together a basic list of what you want: number of attendees, number of meeting rooms, number of meals, and rental equipment. Send an identical list to the hotels/motels you have selected.

Even a small group of 15 to 20 people can negotiate a few extras such as an upgraded room or reduced rates, free coffee, a free meal to offer as a door-prize or in an early-registration drawing. Remember, if you don't ask, they won't volunteer.

The larger your group, the better your negotiating position. You can try to negotiate for free guest rooms or meals for your speakers, meeting rooms, facilities for a welcoming reception, equipment, free or reduced-rate parking, flowers, balloons, decorations—anything the hotel/motel offers as a regular service.

Blocking Rooms

If you are holding all your events at one hotel/motel, another alternative is to block rooms. You should be able to get special rates depending on the number of people you expect.

Be careful about signing contracts. You may find yourself paying for rooms whether they're occupied or not. I know I'm repeating myself, but spending the money to check with a lawyer may save you money later. Establish a cancellation date to release yourself from the contract without penalties.

The hotel will give you an account number for attendees to use to get special rates and confirm they are with your party. When blocking rooms, hotels may give you freebies such as a free or upgraded room for the organizer or free use of a lounge or meeting rooms.

Clarify

Spell out, in writing, exactly what the hotel is providing and at what cost.

- Establish a procedure for people arriving early or staying late.
- Establish a cancellation policy for individual rooms, meals, or the entire event.
- Establish check-in and check-out times.
- Verify the dates.
- Establish how to handle over-booking on your part. You don't want to pay for extra rooms or meals.

Same Last Name

Warn reservations clerks to monitor carefully. When several hundred people are checking in—all with the same last name—extra care is essential!

Accommodations List

If you decide a historic family location is more important than centralized accommodations in a larger city, you will need to supply attendees with a list of overnight facilities in the area.

Ask the local Chamber of Commerce for a list of recommended hotels, motels, college dorms, and campgrounds. You can supplement this list with information from the American Automobile Association (AAA).

Many retirees are campers and will want campground information. You can obtain this from the Chamber of Commerce or from one of several campground directories available at public libraries or AAA. You will want to include the name, directions, number of sites, type of hookups available, recreational activities, and prices. Group camping areas are available at many campgrounds.

Many colleges will rent dormitory rooms during the summer. Rates are as low as $18 for a single room including linens (as of the date of this publication). They will also rent meeting rooms.

Once your list is compiled, call each place to confirm information: name, location, directions, facilities, prices, phone number.

When you create your final accommodations list, state that current prices and information are subject to change. State that attendees are responsible for making their own reservations, confirming information, and paying all charges. <u>Include a disclaimer regarding proofreading and accuracy</u>.

Transportation

First you must decide if you want to arrange transportation for people arriving from out of town or have them take care of it themselves.

Holding your reunion at a hotel simplifies matters, because most hotels provide transportation from the airport for guests.

If you are holding your reunion in several locations, it may make life easier to arrange for group transportation.

The least expensive means of providing transportation is to ask family members living in the area to adopt an out-of-town family and be responsible for getting them to activities.

Buses accommodate the most people—usually 44 people per bus. Check your Yellow Pages for bus companies.

School buses work out very well for short trips. They do not have air conditioning or restrooms. Schools will rent just the buses if you have qualified drivers in your group.

For longer trips, I would suggest regular tour buses for comfort and restrooms.

For small groups, consider a limousine service.

Airlines

Large reunion groups can make deals for reduced ticket rates with the airlines of their choice. If enough tickets are purchased, freebies may be available—ask!

800 Numbers

Nearly all major hotels, motels, and airlines have tool-free telephone numbers. You can get these numbers by calling information:

1-800-555-1212

As of the date of this publication, there is no charge for calling this number. Published directories of 800 numbers are available for sale. Call your local telephone carrier for information.

PROMOTING THE EVENT

"An agreeable feature of the assembly was the attendance of so many characteristic 'old folks,' full of lore, whose combined years would equal those of any one of the ancient patriarchs, thus maintaining the credit of a family somewhat noted for longevity in all its branches."

Now is the time to pull out all the stops—jazz it up! Let people know someone is working behind the scenes. Let them know you are busy planning a reunion that they can't afford to miss!

If you are planning a backyard picnic or a picnic in a public park, you may just plan to send invitations. You still want a jazzy invitation. Use colored paper, use pictures, and use your imagination!

Some families with an interest in genealogy have formed family associations which can afford personalized stationery. Some families can afford to go to a printer and have engraved invitations made up. Handwritten invitations can be a bit more personal.

Whichever you choose, a first-class envelope gets more attention than bulk mail or a postcard. A stamped envelope gets more attention than those going through a postal machine. Return-address labels or a rubber stamp displaying the family name is worth the investment.

Follow up your invitations with a second—and perhaps a third—letter to those who don't respond. For the Hackleman reunion, I put a different picture on each letter's registration forms so that I could tell which letter people responded to. I tabulated the responses and found the following:

1st letter. . . . . . . .48% of registrations

2nd letter. . . . . . . .33% of registrations

3rd letter* . . . . 8% of registrations

Walk-ins. . . . . .11% of registrations

*Sent only to those who indicated an interest in attending.

For a large reunion, you can buy pre-stamped envelopes from the post office and have them delivered to your door. The minimum quantity is 500. You should be able to mail five sheets of 20-pound paper with one first-class stamp.

As of the date of this publication, the cost of offset printing 200 pages (printed both sides) is about $12.

First Promotional Letter

Once you have decided on a schedule of events and made all the necessary arrangements, you are ready to send out your first promotional letter. This should include the following information:

- Date
- Place
- Names, addresses, and telephone numbers of organizers
- Sources of information about accommodations

- Location of facilities
- Details about meals
- Disclaimer: reserve the right to make meal substitutions of equal quality.
- List of other restaurants available for meals not included in your package (can be obtained from Chamber of Commerce)
- Arrangements you have made for a photographer, videographer
- Information on how the family influenced the settling of the reunion location (buildings, churches, original homes, and places of business associated with the family)
- A list of genealogical research facilities in the area
- Type of weather to be expected (AAA guidebooks publish a chart of average temperatures.)
- Suggestions for clothing—casual, formal, costumes
- County, city, and specific location maps
  —Chamber of Commerce can help you get permission to photocopy or provide you with maps themselves
  —Draw arrows on the maps to indicate best routes to specific locations
  —Mark points of interest: farms, cemeteries, historic markers
  —Circle or otherwise mark meeting places, restaurants
- Requests for volunteers to—
  —Make certificates
  —Make name tags
  —Help with registration
  —Organize displays
  —Make or purchase decorations
  —Provide refreshments
  —Arrange transportation
  —Help setup
  —Help cleanup

-Write reunion and/or genealogical
  summary
-Organize activities for children
-Bring a copier and paper
- Suggestions for displays
- Schedule (preliminary—can be expanded for
  confirmation letter)
- List of area attractions (Chamber of
  Commerce will be happy to provide you
  with brochures.)
- Registration form (should include
  deadline for registration and statement
  of cancellation and refund policy)
- List of exactly what the registration fee
  includes

I purchased some Dover Clip Art books
with copyright-free artwork and "dressed up"
my letter with pictures of old-time modes of
transportation.

Second Promotional Letter

Using clip art (USAMAP.WPG) that came
with WordPerfect 5.1, I printed out a map of
the United States (see Appendix, page 115).
Then, using two different styles, I filled in
the states representing 1) reservations
received, representing number of families and
2) Letters of Intent representing number of
families.

For this letter, I again used clipart to
maintain the same theme of old-time
transportation. I dropped the list of area
restaurants, the information about how the
family influenced the settling of the area,
and the suggestions for displays from the
first promotional letter. I adjusted the
information under volunteers to thank those

who had already volunteered, and listed the volunteers still needed. Finally, I added information about area events concurrent to the reunion.

Third Promotional Letter

This was a limited mailing. I sent this letter only to people who said they were interested in coming but who hadn't yet registered—the procrastinators.

This letter included the following information:

- U.S. map showing how many attendees from which states
- Deadline for registration prominently on front page
- Prominent final-notice statement
- Finalized schedule
- Description os souvenirs (Include artwork or photo if available.)
- Descriptions of meals
- Volunteers (Thank those who have volunteered and list jobs still available.)
- Registration form
- Detailed breakdown of exactly what the registration fee includes

You may also want to repeat information about displays, photographer, lodging, weather, and clothing.

Advertising

If you are ready to expand your reunion, consider advertising in a major genealogical

magazine.   This may reach people you don't
even know.

Press Releases

When you write your press release,
remember to tell: WHO, WHAT, WHEN, WHERE, and
HOW. Newspapers prefer a typed, double-spaced
article. Ask the newspaper for the name of
an individual or a department where you should
direct your information. Ask if they will use
a photograph if you provide one.   They will
prefer a black-and-white, glossy photograph.

Edit your press release so that after the
reunion, people can take it to their hometown
newspaper.   Include it in their registration
packages.

The following instructions accompanied
the press release: Please feel free to make
additions or changes as needed. Fill in the
blank spaces with your full name, the names of
those who attended with you, and where you
live. If you have a black-and-white photo of
yourself or an ancestor, the paper may publish
it in conjunction with the article.

COVER LETTER FOR PRESS RELEASE

                              Your Name
                              Full Address
                              Telephone Number

Date:

ATTN: News Director

RE: Your family's reunion
     Dates of event
     Location

Dear Director:

I am enclosing a schedule for the
_____ Family Reunion for your
consideration.

People attending from your area are:

List of names and addresses

For further information, contact:
   Name
   Address
   Telephone Number

                              Sincerely,

                              Your name
                              Committee Title

SAMPLE PRESS RELEASE

NATIONAL HACKLEMAN REUNION

The first National Hackleman Reunion was held August 9, 10, and 11, 1991, in Rushville, Indiana. _____ of _____, and _____ of _____ attended this historic event.

Michael Hackleman was the first Hackleman to come to this country in 1749, settling in Bucks County, Pennsylvania. Michael bound himself to a Pennsylvania farmer for three years to pay his passage, clearing 36 acres of land to square his account.

Michael and his wife, Elisabeth, moved to North Carolina in 1768, then Abbeville District, South Carolina, by 1787. Of Michael's several children, only two, Jacob and George, married and had children of their own.

George remained in the south, migrating to Mississippi. Jacob followed the Cumberland trail north to Indiana Territory in 1804, settling in Rush County, Indiana, as soon as that county was opened to settlers in 1821.

The reunion was a three-day event starting with registration Friday afternoon at the Rushville Public Library. Immediately old photographs, documents, and family Bibles were taken out to be shared. This was followed by a banquet, Friday evening. Jim Scott gave a presentation on how the Hackleman family influenced the settling of Rush County. Linda Moster, of the local D.A.R., accepted donations for the Hackleman cabin, birthplace of Brig. Gen. Pleasant Adams Hackleman, the only Indiana general killed in the Civil War.

A picnic was held on Saturday at the Rush County fairgrounds, and group photographs were taken in front of the Hackleman cabin.

The Hackleman family helped found the Little Flat Rock Baptist Church, now known as the Little Flat Rock Christian Church. Rev. Sargent held special services and the ladies of the church prepared a luncheon, which was served at the Lions Club. Francis Norris spoke on the church and its history.

As the average family grows smaller, extended family ties have become more important. This event brought together fifty Hackleman families from nineteen states located through genealogical research—families that would never have known about each other had they not taken an interest in their heritage.

SOUVENIRS AND FUND-RAISERS

"Be that as it may, among old and young, a current of good feeling pervaded the throng, and coursing warmly through so many veins derived unquestionably a certain quality from its distant source, the kindly heart of the original DANIEL. If little were known of him, the sure tradition that he possessed a loving soul, was better than that of historic deeds without virtue."

I received a postcard from Virginia Howells after the Hackleman reunion. It read: "Every time I have coffee out of my Hackleman coffee cup I remember what a great time we had."

Professional Souvenirs

Souvenir companies publish catalogs filled with hundreds of items you can have personalized for your reunion. Some popular items are coffee mugs, plaques, T-shirts, hats, Frisbees, and key chains.

Your local Better Business Bureau or Chamber of Commerce can help you to find a company in your area. Check with your friends and business associates for companies they have dealt with.

Business and computer shows often have vendors displaying sample items for sale. Shop around for the best price.

You will have to decide whether or not to include the cost in your registration fee. You will need money for the deposit, which is usually at least half the total cost of the souvenirs. Payment in full will be due on receipt. If your family has a treasury fund available, you may be able to use this fund to buy the souvenirs. Then you can take the souvenirs to the reunion and sell them.

Be sure to ask the following questions when ordering souvenirs:

- Are there charges for screening artwork?
- Are there additional charges for more than one color?
- Will the manufacturer guarantee colors? Does it cost extra?
- Who pays shipping charges? How much are they?
- Who pays UPS repacking charges, if incurred?
- Will the manufacturer show a proof to make sure the product is what you want?

A commercial artist can create artwork for you. The cost varies with the complexity of the design. I have had several designs created. They averaged $150.00. It is extremely helpful if you can provide photographs for the artist to work with.

Souvenir companies have artists on staff. Find out how much they charge. Insist on approving the artwork; don't accept it without seeing it.

In the fine print of your contract, is the term "10-percent overrun." This means the manufacturer can make 10-percent more of whatever you order. For instance, to get the lowest price on coffee mugs, I had to order a minimum of 144 mugs. The manufacturer included "10-percent overrun" in the contract, which meant I had to pay for 15 extra mugs whether I wanted them or not. They shipped me 160 mugs I paid for 159—after all, there was a principal at stake.

Do-It-Yourself Souvenirs

You may decide you want something more personal to commemorate your event.

You can purchase plain white T-shirts or sweatshirts and decorate them in the design of your choice with fabric paint or embroidery.

Perhaps someone in your group can make campaign-style buttons. Use miniature family trees or photocopies of a common ancestor's photograph.

Local Souvenirs

What product is native to the reunion location—maple syrup, saltwater taffy, wine? Any of these items would make an excellent choice for a souvenir.

Fund-Raisers

Fund-raisers can take many forms— spaghetti suppers, candy, or baked-good sales.

Souvenirs, especially T-shirts, caps, and coffee mugs displaying the reunion theme or slogan, are good sellers. Souvenir companies can provide you with a catalog. Souvenirs with a date or location on them can be difficult to get rid of after the reunion. Souvenirs without a date can carry over to the next reunion.

Some special ideas come to mind for a family reunion. Conduct an auction with donations from family members—an old-fashioned white-elephant sale.

Sell newsletters. Thelma Landrum, of Columbus, Georgia, collects material and newspaper articles to produce an annual newsletter for the Clemmons family. She bases the price on the number of pages for that year.

Sell souvenir booklets. Include information about the reunion, the program, a list of attendees, genealogical information, or color copies of photographs. You can sell advertising space to family members for congratulatory messages.

Family cookbooks or crafts made by family members are usually best sellers.

Built-in Fund-Raisers

Add a small amount to your registration fee specifically to raise money.

PHOTOGRAPHER, VIDEOGRAPHER, OR BOTH?

"For amid diversities and modifications, resulting from intermarriages and other causes, perhaps the curious observer might be able to detect among the throng some general resemblances, as there were no doubt physiognomical features, as well as mental traits, carried down from age to age and from generation to generation."

Nothing is more valued to a genealogist than an old family photograph, unless it is an old family photograph with the family name on the back.

Hiring a photographer or a videographer to record your reunion will create a tangible memory for generations of your descendants.

Before you hire a photographer or a videographer, ask to see a portfolio. Compare prices. You will want a number of copies, so ask for a quantity discount.

Establish a method of taking orders. Establish how and when the photographs will be delivered. Decide whether you want color or black-and-white prints.

You may want to include the price of one group photograph, postage, and handling in your registration fee. Then you can establish a method of ordering additional copies at extra cost.

To avoid misunderstandings, write up an agreement with the dates, location, and terms.

How Can You Help the Photographer?

You can be sure that someone will have to leave early to catch a plane, so schedule the photo session as early in your program as possible.

Decide on a background for your photograph—an old family home, a cemetery, a stage. If you are planning an outdoor photo, be prepared with a "rain date" or an alternate location.

Depending on the size of your group, you will need to round up chairs, benches, or bleachers.

Group photos take time. Plan at least an hour. While you're planning this time slot, don't forget to allow plenty of time for people to get from the preceding event to the photo session.

Groups of More Than 50 People

For a group this size, I recommend hiring a professional portrait photographer. Professionals use a $2\frac{1}{4}$ inch film format instead of 35 mm. This gives you the quality you will need in 11 x 14-inch or 16 x 20-inch enlargements made from the negatives.

Video Interviews

Video interviews are terrific—especially if they are not too lengthy! You want to get everyone on one tape.

I recommend that you provide a list of

questions in the registration packages so that people will have a chance to think about their answers.

Provide the person doing the interviews with a checklist of people to interview.

Try to find out something personal about people before the interviews—hobbies, business interests, a special project or program. Armed with this information, you can prompt them and get them to talk more freely about themselves.

Ask several or all of the interviewees a trick question—for instance "What is your lineage?" Or have them tell you about a specific famous person in your family. Then edit the responses together.

There is no such thing as a quiet place during a family reunion. Everyone is talking at once. You can, however, control other noises by turning off appliances or fans.

You will need to reach a clear agreement with the videographer on who will be responsible for duplicating, packaging, and shipping.

Video Family History

You can, of course, use the video interview to gather extensive family history. Audio or videotape is still the best method for accuracy and speed. The tapes can be transcribed at a later date. Professional services will even transcribe tapes for you—at a price, of course.

If you choose this lengthier type of interview, I suggest you lay out a complete list of questions beginning with name, birth date and place of birth, and then work forward through the school years, college, career, marriage, and children. Personally, I like to add hobbies, family stories, church affiliations, volunteer activities, and professional associations.

Reunion Video

You may want to create a reunion video covering all the events. To make a memorable video, include a few extras:

- "Welcome to Our City" sign
- Local points of interest
- Courthouse
- Family home
- Cemetery gates, tombstones
- Historic markers
- Entrance to the hotel/motel
- Places of historical interest mentioned by a guest speaker

Ask your guest speakers if you may videotape their talks.

While we were doing our group photograph, I took a tape recorder and asked all the attendees to give me their names. The original purpose was to identify people in the photograph. But then when we produced our reunion video, we were able to include a video shot of the group gathering for the photograph with people calling out their names.

TIP: Don't forget those microphones and extra batteries.

SAMPLE INTERVIEW QUESTIONS

Sometime during the picnic on Saturday and again during lunch on Sunday, Hackleman descendants will be approached by a video camera— PLEASE DON'T RUN.

We are providing you with an advance copy of the questions to be asked to give you some time to think.   You may want to make some notes or even write a paragraph or two.   Then if you are camera-shy or have lost your short-term memory like the rest of us, you can just read your notes to the camera!

- Name?

- When and where were you born?

- Who are your parents?

- Where do you live now?

- How did your family happen to settle where you are now living?

- Where did you go to school, college?

- Occupation?

- What hobbies do you enjoy?

- Who is your favorite ancestor and why?

- Tell a favorite story about yourself.

- Tell a favorite story about your immediate family.

- Tell a favorite story about your parents.

- Tell a favorite story about your grandparents.

Please feel free to eliminate or substitute your own questions for any of the questions above.   Just tell the interviewer ahead of time.

REGISTRATION

"In the family now met, it is believed that no inheritance has been stronger or more decided than the love of kindred."

Registration sets the tone for the whole reunion. It can occur before or during the Welcoming Reception.

Registration for a backyard picnic may require only a sign-up sheet.

As your reunion grows, so does registration. Arrange your registration tables by family branches or alphabetically. Post large signs where they can be seen easily. Use large print.

For a large reunion, it will be helpful to have one or two people explaining the system and helping people get into the proper lines. Have all the volunteers wear badges, hats, or T-shirts for easy identification.

If you are holding registration at your host hotel or motel, work with the management. More than one group may want to use the lobby.

Set up your registration tables so that registration flows from one end to the other. If you plan to serve refreshments during registration, put them in a separate area, and put your tables for displays as far away from the refreshment tables as possible. At the Hackleman reunion, most people were extremely careful around the displays. However, one lady nearly gave me heart failure by setting her coffee cup down near irreplaceable old photographs on the table.

You will also need a table for selling items such as extra souvenirs, fund-raising mementos, books, and photographs.

You must decide whether to pre-assemble registration packages or use the pickup system. Pre-assembly requires work ahead of time, but, saves valuable time during registration, especially when large numbers of people must move through the area quickly.

After receiving their packages, people move down the table to pick up their souvenirs and information from the Chamber of Commerce.

If souvenirs are included in the registration fee, assign someone to check names off a prepared list to make sure everyone gets the right number. Another volunteer should take charge of selling extras. You will need a money box and change.

Believe it or not, you will need a table to handle walk-in registrations.

Two or three hours is more than enough time to hold registration.

A sizable number of people did not pick up their packages at the Hackleman Welcoming Reception and Registration. They waited until the banquet that night, making it extremely inconvenient for the registration committee. Because we had to set up a makeshift registration table in a small corner of the restaurant, we did not have any time to visit with people and had scarcely enough time to eat! Be prepared for this kind of difficulty.

Name Tags

If I learned anything during my days with the Cub Scouts, I learned that name tags can be made out of virtually anything—in an infinite number of shapes. Your imagination is your only limitation.

If you use computer-generated name tags, make duplicates and use them for the outside of your registration packages. A third copy can be used for door-prize tickets.

Extra name tags can also serve as admission devices for meals and events.

You can create name tags in several ways. They can be handwritten, typed, professionally printed, or created on a computer. Perhaps there is a calligrapher among your attendees.

Please, use large lettering for those of us with bifocals.

In addition to each person's name, include the home city and state.

Have a supply of blank name tags on hand for walk-in registrations.

By the second day of the Hackleman reunion, I noticed people were writing their lineages on their name tags. Perhaps you could use different colors for each branch of the family.

Someone suggested color-coded name tags to identify family branches. This would make finding other members of the same branch very easy.

Another suggestion is to include in the registration package T-shirts in different colors for different branches of the family.

Adhesive name tags seldom last through a single day. At the time of this publication, badge holders with clips come in boxes of 100 for about $10.00.

Registration packages should include the following:

- Reunion program
- Meal tickets
- Name tags
- List of attendees and addresses
- Maps: county, local, city, specific*
- Brochures on local attractions
- Information about area historical locations associated with your surname
- Agenda for business meeting
- Press release
- Door-prize tickets
- List of local courthouse and libraries including their hours of operation (for people who forgot to pack theirs)
- Interview questions
- Event tickets
- Pad/paper*
- Pen/pencils*
- Tourist information: shopping, restaurants, nightclubs
- Evaluation forms
- Emergency numbers for hospital, ambulance, and police

*Ask the Chamber of Commerce and local businesses to donate some of these items.

BUILDING A GENEALOGY

"Facts too and incidents in the lives of obscurest individuals frequently serve to illustrate the times, impart a hue to a broader page, and furnish a hint in the generalizations of history. We may regard it, then, as a favorable omen, if an increasing taste is manifest for a line of studies hitherto neglected, if genealogies are traced with scrupulous care, and family gatherings, sometimes on an extensive scale, including branches and alliances, are not uncommon. They conduce to strengthen the bonds of fellowship among those of the same blood, to rivet firmly some links in a broken chain, and to add a little to the stock of fading reminisces [sic]."

Hosting a reunion offers an ideal opportunity to start building a genealogy.

Sign-Up Sheets

Your sign-up sheet is a genealogical beginning—make the most of it.

If your group is large enough, have several sign-up sheets—one for each family branch. Ask for full name, current address, and telephone number.

Request for Information

Another means of collecting information is to include a Request for Information form with your confirmation letter. Keep it simple. In addition to names, ask for birth, death, and marriage dates and places.

You may also be able to get some biographical information by asking specific questions: "What is your occupation?" "What hobbies do you enjoy?"

Another alternative is to leave room on the Request for Information form and ask individuals to write a biography. Make it a small space. Too much space scares people and they won't write anything. Suggest that they attach additional sheets if they need more space.

Inevitably some folks will not return the form. Compile a list of these people, and then ask a volunteer to take blank forms and interview them at the reunion.

Research Center

Assign one or more volunteers to go through family Bibles and records on the display tables and copy all pertinent information. We were fortunate to have a family with an office in their camper, which included a computer and a copier.

Family Medical Tree

Ask people to write down their medical family trees. This information is becoming more and more important to future generations.

Summary

Write up a summary of the information you collect. Include names, addresses, dates, biographical information, and relationships. Ask for permission before publishing telephone numbers.

I would like to suggest sending a copy to a State Archives or other genealogical society

connected to your family. Genealogists
researching your family name will appreciate
finding this information. Be sure to include
the name and address of a contact.

Take a copy to your next reunion and keep
adding to it.

DISPLAYS AND DECORATIONS

"While some then were pleasantly engaged with the forementioned 'old folks,' in tracing the line of their descent from one or another of his seven sons, others drew a whiff from the identical tobacco-pipe used by our progenitor, though in the troubled days when he smoked it, and the aboriginal tribes in his neighborhood were far from friendly, it could hardly be called the 'calumet of peace.' It was of iron with a thin stem and a delicately small bowl, indicating either that he was not an inordinate devotee, or that the 'weed,' which is even costly still, was then somewhat precious, perhaps only less so than the refreshing herb imbibed out of marvelously small cups at a later period. Likewise the China punch-bowl which our good ancestor had brought with him from the 'old county,' had been carefully preserved and handed down as an heir loom. This bowl, like the bowl of the pipe, was by no means capacious. "

Displays

Provide tables for people to set up their photo albums, dishes, medals, buttons, and whatever else they bring to share. You can buy paper tablecloths from your local grocery store or your local paper outlet store. I suggest you ask someone to supervise the display tables.

Make a display out of your sign-up sheet. Using a large sheet of construction paper, create a basic family tree. Run colored string, ribbon, or yarn from each family branch to separate sign-up sheets.

When creating displays, consider how you are going to present them. A picnic pavilion may not have walls. If you do have a facility with walls, are you allowed to use tacks, nails, tape, or plastic adhesive?

You can make an inexpensive stand to place on a table or the ground by using utility board. Cut three equal pieces. Bind the sides together by threading string through the holes. Voila!

My father-in-law, Burr K. Hackleman of Vandalia, Illinois, designed an adjustable lineage chart to show the relationships between attendees.

He purchased lightweight white poster board and cut it into 2 x 13 strips. Then he measured off 1-inch blocks down the 13-inch side. The top block he left blank. In the second block, he wrote the descendant's name and current residence (city and state). In the third block, he entered the earliest known ancestor, year of birth and death, and wife's name. He continued the lineage down to the current generation. The bottom block he left blank.

Next he cut several 13 x 24-inch pieces of poster board and several 1 x 24-strips. By attaching the strips to the top and bottom of the large pieces he created pockets. Just before the reunion, he slipped the lineage charts into the pockets in genealogical order. This was not an easy task, because we all tried our hand at upsetting his stack of charts while he did his best to protect his work! We used plastic adhesive to hang the boards on a long wall at the library during registration and carried it over to the pavilion at the fairgrounds where we held our picnic. It was a very popular display.

CAUTION: Cover your displays with plastic or post someone to watch over them. Some people will put coffee cups down anywhere!

Decorations

Decorate everything—the house, porch, fence, pavilion, or hall. Do it simply with handmade signs, crepe paper, balloons, and/or flowers from your garden.

Several very good computer software programs can produce banners and signs. These programs usually have copyright-free clip art that you can use to "dress up" your signs with graphics.

If you have the funds for imprinted items, go to a wedding-supply store. These stores also have a large selection of table favors.

CAUTION: Don't forget to ask if you can use tacks, nails, tape, or plastic adhesive.

Themes

Just for fun, select a decorating theme for your reunion. Coordinate it with your program theme if you have one.

My in-laws, Burr and Mildred Hackleman, quite by accident selected Friday the 13th for their wedding date. Told it was bad luck to change the date after setting it, they decided to have fun with it. They put a ladder over the entrance to the house, invited a black cat

Front view, Brig. Gen. P.A. Hackleman medallion. Medal courtesy of June Gardner of Tolono, Illinois. Photo courtesy B. Keith Hackleman, photographer.

Back view, Brig. Gen. P.A. Hackleman medallion. Medal courtesy of June Gardner of Tolono, Illinois. Photo courtesy of B. Keith Hackleman, photographer.

who curled up next to the minister and slept,
and were married at precisely 1:13 p.m. (13th
hour, 13th minute) under a floral umbrella.

So for their 50th wedding anniversary, we
duplicated all the trimmings. We bought an
earring ladder for the top of the cake,
propped ladders up by all the doors, and set
black cats (the stuffed variety) around the
house.

If you're not into tempting fate, you may
want to do something a little more
traditional.

FINISHING TOUCHES

"To be conscious of no ties is to lose one of the most genial incentives to human action, and he is not to be envied who can mingle in such groups as we have named, without a sentiment that is ennobling."

Certificates

Blank certificates are fairly inexpensive and are available in stationery stores. The information you fill in can be typed or handwritten. Ask around for a family member who does calligraphy.

You can also create certificates with a computer program.

You can give a simple Certificate of Attendance to everyone, but put your imagination to work. Create unique certificates for your family members. They can be funny or serious.

You can make certificates for the oldest, the youngest, the family who brought the most children, and the attendee who traveled farthest to get to the reunion.

We gave a certificate to the person who traveled the most circuitous route (CA-IL-NY-MA-IL-AR-IN) to the reunion, and another to the couple with a computer and copier in their camper.

Give certificates for achievement such as scholarship, graduating from high school or college, community work, or church activities. Find out who works with the Red Cross or volunteers with the Boy Scouts or Girl Scouts.

Have blank certificates on hand at the reunion for last-minute presentations. We gave certificates for the "best use of a broom" and "best use of garden tools." We gave certificates to those who helped set up tables and take them down.

The important factor is to give recognition to those people who cared enough to come.

Door Prizes

Door prizes offer a fun way to share. For the Hackleman reunion, I took bottles of New York State wine. Russ and Beverly Hackleman, of Oregon, brought special jars of homemade jelly. The Rushville Chamber of Commerce donated lapel pins and coasters. To avoid the expense of mailing door prizes, be sure to specify "must be present to win."

Garden Tools

When we visited Rushville, Indiana, the year before the reunion, we noticed that the Hackleman cabin needed cleaning up. At reunion time, we came prepared with a broom to sweep out the cabin and garden tools for sprucing up the grounds. We planned to do the work ourselves, but other family members quickly volunteered to help.

Road Signs

Make and put up road signs with directions or arrows. Use large print in black or dark blue ink. Most of us wear glasses!

After the Reunion

When the reunion is over, it's time to write a summary of your gathering. Include the date, location, names of attendees, names of committee members, money raised for your specific project, names of guests, and guest-speaker topics.

You may want to combine this information with the genealogical information you collected into one booklet or newsletter. Take copies to your next reunion, and sell them as souvenirs.

Gather up the evaluation sheets that people mailed to you after the reunion. What did they like? What didn't they like? What suggestions did they make for the next reunion?

This is also the time to write down what you felt went wrong. Makes notes on changes you would make. Pass this information along to the person planning the next reunion.

When my family and I started going on camping trips, I wasn't sure what to pack. After each trip, I made a list of what I used, what I didn't use, and what I wished I had taken along. I filed the list, and the next time we went camping I was better prepared.

The same technique will help you or your successor plan a better reunion.

Thank-You Notes

Send thank-you notes or letters to *everyone* who helped you put the reunion together.

You can go a step further by sending notes to everyone who attended. If your reunion was small, notes can be handwritten. If it was large, I suggest you have cards printed.

CHECKLIST FOR PACKING

- Checkbook
- Extra registration forms
- Registration packages
- Extra meal tickets
- Extra name-tags
- Extra name-tag holders
- Extra door-prize tickets
- Souvenirs
- Money box with change
- Decorations
- Blank paper
- Scotch tape
- Masking tape
- Thumbtacks
- Plastic adhesive (Plastitak/Fun-tak)
- Stapler
- Extra staples
- Paper clips
- Rubber bands
- Pens
- Pencils
- Correction fluid (Wite-Out or Liquid Paper)
- Copies of canceled checks and correspondence confirming meals, facilities, and speakers
- First-aid kit
- Small tool chest with hammer, nails, pliers, screwdriver

EPILOGUE

"I also hope that this reunion of the family will serve to make some friends who are now strangers, and increase their interest in the name, and their veneration for the founder of the family."

Now that you have gathered around the old hearth-stones with your family, you will always hold the memory with you.

You have met strangers and made new friends from around the country. You have strengthened your family ties, and now belong to something unique— your extended family.

I leave you with a few quotes from the video interviews my husband and I did at the Hackleman reunion:

"I love all my new cousins." DOLORES WALTZ, Elwood, IN.

"It has been my pleasure to become acquainted with Hacklemans and this gives spur to widening our acquaintance among the family."
JUNE GARDNER, Tolono, IL.

"This has really been a great, great experience for all of us to get together and find out about the rest of the family, see the cabin, and the places where our ancestors have been." BETTY ANDERSON, Torrington, WY.

"I especially appreciate the fact that we were able to have the reunion in this neighborhood with its historical context and have a chance to worship together in church this morning. It's just nice to see so many people with the name spelled correctly." JAY RUSSELL HACKLEMAN, Grosse Pointe Park, MI.

HACKLEMAN ASSOCIATES

Phyllis A. Hackleman
25 Lake View Terrace
Rochester, New York 14613
Telephone: 716-458-0386

Specializing in Preparation of Genealogical Manuscripts

October 5, 1990

W A G O N S   H O !

NATIONAL HACKLEMAN REUNION

AUGUST 9, 10, 11--1991

RUSHVILLE, INDIANA

The votes were tabulated and 62% of you voted for Rushville, Indiana, 68% voted for an area of historical significance, and 65% voted for August.

Mildred, Burr, Keith and I made a flying trip to Rushville, Indiana this past August 15th and 16th. We were welcomed with open arms and treated to the most wonderful hospitality, thanks mostly to the efforts of Linda Moster of the local D.A.R. She notified everyone she thought we might need to see and everybody was waiting for us--the Rushville Public Library had books pulled out, the caterers had menu suggestions, the Chamber of Commerce made up a list of recommended local hotels and campgrounds. Linda greeted us at our hotel with a tray of fruit, nuts, chips and soda. She made arrangements to open up Gen. Hackleman's cabin, her husband helped us contact the minister at the Little Flat Rock Christian Church, recommended a guest speaker, and treated us to dinner at her home that evening. In less that 24 hours we were able to arrange almost everything we needed.

W H E R E   T O   S T A Y

Hotel space in Rushville is limited; however, there are several fine places with a 17 mile radius. A four page guide to local hotels, campgrounds, bed and breakfasts is available by sending a stamped, self-addressed envelope to:

Hackleman Associates
25 Lake View Terrace
Rochester, New York 14613-1710

M E A L S

Friday night's buffet at Winkerby's includes roast beef, ham, fried chicken, potatoes, salad, vegetables, beverage, desert, tax and gratuity. Winkerby's is air-conditioned.

Saturday's catered picnic includes hot dogs, hamburgers, BBQ chicken, potato salad, macaroni salad, baked beans, chips, brownies, cookies, beverages, tax and gratuity. It is being catered by Winkerby's.

Sunday's lunch is being prepared by the Little Flat Rock Christian Church's ladies guild and includes meat, potatoes, salad, beverages, desert, tax and gratuity.

*****Winkerby's and the Little Flat Rock Christian Church reserve the right to make changes of equal value and quality if necessary.

----------:----------

Rushville has a McDonalds, Burger King, Pizza Hut and several family style restaurants for meals not included in the registration fee.

P I C N I C

The Root Memorial Building can be closed up in the event of rain or opened up in the event of hot weather.

It is located on the fairgrounds on the north side of town. There are ball fields, tennis, and swimming available-- so bring your bats, balls, and swimming trunks.

The Hackleman cabin is located just a few yards from the picnic pavilion. It will be open for those that would like to see the inside.

P H O T O G R A P H E R

We are making arrangements for a group photograph to be taken Saturday afternoon. This photo will be offered for sale at the lowest possible price we can manage. The photographer (my husband, M.F.A., photography) will be available Saturday afternoon if you would like other photos taken.

RESEARCH OPPORTUNITIES

Indiana is rich in Hackleman family history. In 1803 Jacob[2] Hackleman (Michael[1]) came to Indiana Territory by packhorse. By 1806, all of his 14 children and their spouses had joined Jacob. From here the family grew and spread throughout Indiana and began the trek west.

Since whole families picked up and moved together, Indiana is also rich in Tyner, Perkins, Milner, Sailors, Osborn, Hawkins, Lines, Robinson, Adams, Williams, Webb, Allensworth, and Davis history.

You will want to plan enough time to visit the libraries in Rushville, Connersville and Brookville. You may also want to visit the State Archives in Indianapolis and the outstanding genealogical library at Fort Wayne.

Bring your camera. Local county maps make locating cemeteries and churches easy. We will have as many of these maps as we can, available at registration for your convenience.

RUSHVILLE IN AUGUST

The average daily temperatures range from 85^0 during the day to 63^0 of an evening. Winkerby's restaurant is air-conditioned. The Root Memorial Building will provide plenty of shade as well as protection from rain. The Little Flat Rock Christian Church is also air-conditioned.

C O M E   P R E P A R E D

Come prepared for a smooth registration, bring:
* registration confirmation

Come prepared to be comfortable, bring:
* comfortable clothes
* comfortable shoes

Come prepared to do research, bring:
* pencils, pens, paper for taking copious notes
* research notes for reference and sharing

Come prepared to have a good time, bring:
* enthusiasm and a sense of humor

V O L U N T E E R S

Since we live so far apart it is nearly impossible to organize committees to help with this or that. If anyone has the time, the following things would be appreciated:

- If someone has a computer with the capacity for making up certificates, it would be great to have certificates for the oldest living family member, the youngest, and whatever else the imagination can come up with.

- Would anyone be willing to make and bring name tags that could be filled out at Registration on Friday? This could be a good project for someone with a Cub Scout den or Brownie troop.

- Would anyone be willing to come early and be part of a welcoming committee at the Rushville Public Library? We could also use help putting up pictures and bios.

- We have the Root Memorial Building reserved for the entire day on Saturday, would someone be willing to organize some games for the children?

- We have reserved the library meeting room from 9am until 5pm including the kitchen facilities so we can make coffee. Would someone be willing to bring some cupcakes or cookies to go with the coffee?

- There may be someone with a need for transportation from their hotel to the various event sites. Is there someone in the Rushville area that would be willing to coordinate any requests we receive with folks with extra room in their cars?

- If you have an idea or project you would like to have included, please write.

D I S P L A Y S

Please bring your photo albums, Bibles, or any other memorabilia you would like to share.

P H O T O S   &   B I O S

We would like to each participate to send us a snapshot of themselves and a short biography. They will be mounted on construction paper and arranged into a display for the reunion.

SCHEDULE

Friday, August 9:

12 noon — 5:00 pm	Registration at the Rushville Public Library. The library opens at 9:00 am for research.
6:00 pm	Buffet dinner at Winkerby's, 205 North Main St.
7:30 pm	Guest speaker, Jim Scott, will share his knowledge of Rush County history.

Saturday, August 10:

2:00 pm — until ?	Catered picnic at the Root Memorial Building at the Fairgrounds, about 50 yards from the Hackleman Cabin.

Sunday, August 11:

10:15 am — 11:30 am	Church services at the Little Flat Rock
12:00 noon	Bon Voyage Luncheon

REGISTRATION   FEES

Registration fees include:

- 3-meat buffet at Winkerby's on Friday evening, August 9
- 3-meat catered picnic at the Root Memorial Bldg., August 10
- Hot lunch on Sunday, August 11
- Each adult, age 18 and over will receive a ceramic coffee mug featuring a line drawing of the Hackleman cabin
- A donation to the Little Flat Rock Christian Church

AREA ATTRACTIONS

One of the most outstanding area attractions is **METAMORA**. Situated on the Whitewater Canal there are steam train rides, canal boat rides, and carriage rides. The shopper will find upward of a hundred small shops to chose from. There are several restaurants to chose from.

Don't miss Whitewater State Park with it's fine fishing, swimming and camping facilities. Experience walking over the same ground your ancestors did as they traveled up the Whitewater valley to settle a new territory!

Come for the "Steam Engine Festival" in Rushville. This festival is held the 1st weekend of August and includes a flea market, entertainment, log splitting contests, broom making, and a parade of steam run vehicles about every two hours. Oh yes, and an Old Calliope! Contact the Rushville Chamber of Commerce: (317) 932-2880.

Knightstown has an Antique mall, 136 W. Carey Street. Over 20,000 sq. feet of diversified stock.

On Carthage Road between Knightstown and Carthage is the Michael Bonne Copper Smith Shop with a 19th century museum workshop.

The Rushville area is home to six covered bridges.

Most of all, bring your notebooks, pencils and walking shoes so you can do "a little research" while you're here. Rushville, Connersville, Liberty, Brookville, and the surrounding area are rich in Hackleman history you won't want to miss!

D.A.R. NEEDS YOUR HELP

The Rushville Chapter of the D.A.R. is asking for donations of replicas--and I stress replicas--of any memorabilia they could use in the Hackleman Cabin. They are not looking for anything irreplaceable or valuable as the cabin has been broken into and vandalized twice. The cabin is rather sparse and they would like to dress it up a bit.

REGISTRATION FORM

The following rates are in effect for reservations received before May 1, 1991.**

			TOTAL
_____	Adults, age 18 and over	$48.00 each*	_____
_____	Child, age 8 to age 17	$35.00 each*	_____
_____	Child, age 4 to age 7	$20.00 each*	_____
_____	Child, age 0 to age 3	No charge	
_____	Extra Coffee Mugs	$ 5.00 each	_____
		TOTAL ENCLOSED	_____

*Add $5.00 per person for reservations received after May 1, 1991

There is a $10.00 cancellation fee per adult, age 18 and over for cancellations received before May 1, 1991. Since there are deposits and guarantees involved there will be **No Refunds for cancellations received after May 1, 1991.

Please print:

Your name: _____

Mailing address: _____

_____

City, State, Zip: _____

Phone #: (   )   _____

Names of other persons for whom you are making reservations:

_____   _____

_____   _____

_____

Please make checks or money orders payable to Hackleman Associates and mail to:

    Hackleman Associates
    25 Lake View Terrace
    Rochester, New York 14613

NATIONAL HACKLEMAN REUNION

AUGUST 9, 10, 11--1991

RUSHVILLE, INDIANA

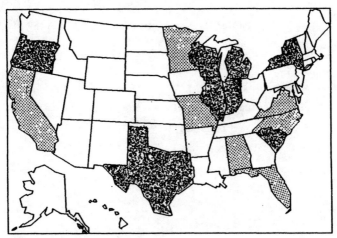

Reservations representing 10 families
"Letters of Intent" representing 13 families

ALL ABOARD !!

The reunion train is on it´s way!   I want to thank all of you
that registered early. I also want to encourage the rest of you to
please register as soon as possible.

August is just around the bend.

S C H E D U L E

Friday, August 9:

12 noon - 5:00 pm   Registration at the Rushville Public Library.
                      The library opens at 9:00 am for research.

6:00 pm
                      Buffet dinner at Winkerby's, 205 North Main St.

7:30 pm
                      Guest speaker, Jim Scott, will share his
                      knowledge of Rush County history.

Saturday, August 10:

2:00 pm - until ?   Catered picnic at the Root Memorial Building
                      at the Fairgrounds, about 50 yards from the
                      Hackleman Cabin.

Sunday, August 11:

10:15 am - 11:30 am   Church services at the Little Flat Rock

12:00 noon   Bon Voyage Luncheon

WHERE TO STAY:

Hotel space in Rushville is limited;
however, there are several fine places
with a 17 mile radius.   A four page
guide to local hotels, campgrounds,
bed and breakfasts is available by
sending a stamped, self-addressed
envelope to:

Hackleman Associates
25 Lake View Terrace
Rochester, New York 14613-1710

RUSHVILLE IN AUGUST

The average daily temperatures range from 85⁰ during the day to 63⁰
of an evening. Winkerby's restaurant is air-conditioned. The Root
Memorial Building will provide plenty of shade as well as
protection from rain.   The Little Flat Rock Christian Church is
also air-conditioned.

A R E A   A T T R A C T I O N S

One of the most outstanding area attractions is **METAMORA**. Situated on the Whitewater Canal there are steam train rides, canal boat rides, and carriage rides. The shopper will find upward of a hundred small shops to chose from. There are several restaurants to chose from.

Don't miss Whitewater State Park with it's fine fishing, swimming and camping facilities. Experience walking over the same ground your ancestors did as they traveled up the Whitewater valley to settle a new territory!

Come for the "Steam Engine Festival" in Rushville. This festival is held the 1st weekend of August and includes a flea market, entertainment, log splitting contests, broom making, and a parade of steam run vehicles about every two hours. Oh yes, and an Old Calliope! Contact the Rushville Chamber of Commerce: (317) 932-2880.

Knightstown has an Antique mall, 136 W. Carey Street. Over 20,000 sq. feet of diversified stock.

On Carthage Road between Knightstown and Carthage is the Michael Bonne Copper Smith Shop with a 19th century museum workshop.

The Rushville area is home to six covered bridges.

Most of all, bring your notebooks, pencils and walking shoes so you can do "a little research" while you're here. Rushville, Connersville, Liberty, Brookville, and the surrounding area are rich in Hackleman history you won't want to miss!

D.A.R. NEEDS YOUR HELP

The Rushville Chapter of the D.A.R. is asking for donations of replicas--and I stress replicas--of any memorabilia they could use in the Hackleman Cabin. They are not looking for anything irreplaceable or valuable as the cabin has been broken into and vandalized twice. The cabin is rather sparse and they would like to dress it up a bit.

FAMILY RESEARCH

During your stay in Indiana, plan to allow time to walk where your ancestors walked.

Jacob Hackleman brought his family to Indiana Territory in 1803. By 1806, all of his 14 children and their spouses had joined Jacob. From here the family grew and spread throughout Indiana and began the trek west.

The libraries in Rushville and the surrounding towns have genealogy departments that can assist you in researching your family. The State Archives in Indianapolis and the Allen Co. Public Library in Fort Wayne both have outstanding genealogy collections.

A list of library hours has been compiled and will be sent to you with your confirmation letter.

Be sure to bring your camera. Local county maps make locating cemeteries and churches easy. We will have as many of these maps as we can, available at registration for your convenience.

LITTLE FLAT ROCK CHRISTIAN CHURCH

From the 150th Anniversary (1830-1980) booklet, *Little Flat Rock Christian Church*: "The parent church from which the Little Flat Rock Christian church originated was the Little Flat Rock Regular Baptist Church, organized in 1821 as an outgrowth of a meeting held in Conrad Sailor's store in April of that year. This Baptist church was the first religious organization in Rush County and was instrumental in establishing churches throughout Rush and surrounding counties."
". . .in consequence of the difference of doctrine, the congregation of the Little Flat Rock Baptist Church, by mutual consent, agreed to divide. The following thirty brethren and sisters obtained their letters of dismissal, which stated they were persons of good moral character, and became charter members of the Little Flat Rock Christian Church: John P. Thompson and Priscilla, his wife; Abner Hackleman and Elizabeth, his wife; Simeon Loyd and Mary, his wife; John Hawkins and Nancy, his wife; John Heaton and Hester, his wife; William Moor and Rebecca, his wife; Phoebe Heaton and Thomas Heaton; Jacob Hackleman; James Frazee and Catherine, his wife; John McDaniel and Catherine, his wife; Jacob Coon and Margaret, his wife; Ebenezer Thompson, Margaret Williams; Rebecca Garrison; Mary McDaniel; Margaret Stephens; Mahala Taylor; Elizabeth Maple; Mary Coon; Elizabeth Moor."

FGS CONFERENCE   **August 15-17, 1991**

The Federation of Genealogical Societies is holding their annual conference in Fort Wayne, Indiana. Top speakers from around the country will present three days of lectures and discussions for both the beginning and experienced researcher. For information write: 1991 FGS Conference, Attn: Curt Witcher, Conference Chair, 900 Webster Street, PO Box 2270, Fort Wayne, In 46801-2270

V O L U N T E E R S

I want to thank those of you that have already volunteered to help. We still need help in the following areas:

• If someone has a computer with the capacity for making up certificates, it would be great to have certificates for the oldest family member attending, the youngest, and whatever else the imagination can come up with.

• We have the Root Memorial Building reserved for the entire day on Saturday, would someone be willing to organize some games for the children?

• We have reserved the library meeting room from 9am until 5pm including the kitchen facilities so we can make coffee. Would someone be willing to bring some cupcakes or cookies to go with the coffee?

• There may be someone with a need for transportation from their hotel to the various event sites. Is there someone in the Rushville area that would be willing to coordinate any requests we receive with folks with extra room in their cars?

PHOTOGRAPHER

We are making arrangements for a group photograph to be taken Saturday afternoon. This photo will be offered for sale at the lowest possible price we can manage. The photographer (my husband, M.F.A., photography) will be available Saturday afternoon if you would like other photos taken.

REGISTRATION FEES

Registration fees include:

- 3-meat buffet at Winkerby's on Friday evening, August 9
- 3-meat catered picnic at the Root Memorial Bldg., August 10
- Hot lunch on Sunday, August 11
- Each adult, age 18 and over will receive a ceramic coffee mug featuring a line drawing of the Hackleman cabin
- A donation to the Little Flat Rock Christian Church

WHAT'S COOKING?

Friday night's buffet at Winkerby's includes roast beef, ham, fried chicken, potatoes, salad, vegetables, beverage, desert, tax and gratuity. Winkerby's is air-conditioned.

Saturday's catered picnic includes hot dogs, hamburgers, BBQ chicken, potato salad, macaroni salad, baked beans, chips, brownies, cookies, beverages, tax and gratuity. It is being catered by Winkerby's.

Sunday's lunch is being prepared by the Little Flat Rock Christian Church's ladies guild and includes meat, potatoes, salad, beverages, desert, tax and gratuity.

*****Winkerby's and the Little Flat Rock Christian Church reserve the right to make changes of equal value and quality if necessary.

----------◆----------

Rushville has a McDonalds, Burger King, Pizza Hut and several family style restaurants for meals not included in the registration fee.

DISPLAYS

Please bring your photo albums, Bibles, or any other memorabilia you would like to share.

PICNIC

The Root Memorial Building can be closed up in the event of rain or opened up in the event of hot weather.

It is located on the fairgrounds on the north side of town. There are ball fields, tennis, and swimming available--so bring your bats, balls, and swimming trunks.

The Hackleman cabin is located just a few yards from the picnic pavilion. It will be open for those that would like to see the inside.

REGISTRATION FORM

The following rates are in effect for reservations received
before May 1, 1991.**

		TOTAL
_____Adults, age 18 and over	$48.00 each*	_____
_____Child, age 8 to age 17	$35.00 each*	_____
_____Child, age 4 to age 7	$20.00 each*	_____
_____Child, age 0 to age 3	No charge	
_____Extra Coffee Mugs	$5.00 each	_____

TOTAL ENCLOSED   _____

*Add $5.00 per person for reservations received after May 1, 1991

**There is a $10.00 cancellation fee per adult, age 18 and over for
cancellations received before May 1, 1991. Since there are
deposits and guarantees involved there will be **No Refunds** for
cancellations received after May 1, 1991.

Please print:

Your name:_____

Mailing address:_____

_____

City, State, Zip:_____

Phone #: (   ) _____

Names of other persons for whom you are making reservations:

_____   _____

_____   _____

_____   _____

Please make checks or money orders
payable to Hackleman Associates
and mail to:

Hackleman Associates
25 Lake View Terrace
Rochester, New York 14613

NATIONAL HACKLEMAN REUNION

AUGUST 9, 10, 11--1991

RUSHVILLE, INDIANA

LET'S GET TOGETHER !!!

August is coming up fast.   Please make your plans to come as soon as possible.

As of May 19, 1991 sixty-three (63) adults from sixteen (16) states have made reservations to attend.

RESERVATIONS MUST BE

RECEIVED BY AUGUST 1, 1991

Since meal counts must be given to the caterers on August 2, 1991, I cannot accept reservations "at the door." If for some reason you cannot return your registration form by August 1, 1991, please call (716) 458-0386 to make other arrangements.

SCHEDULE

Friday, August 9:

12 noon - 5:00 pm	Registration at the Rushville Public Library. The library opens at 9:00 am for research.
6:00 pm	Buffet dinner at Winkerby's, 205 North Main St.
7:30 pm	Guest speaker, Jim Scott, will share his knowledge of Rush County history.

Saturday, August 10:

1:00 pm - 2:00 pm	Business meeting to establish Hackleman Association.
2:00 pm - until ?	Catered picnic at the Root Memorial Building at the Fairgrounds, about 50 yards from the Hackleman Cabin which will be open for visitors.

Sunday, August 11:

10:15 am - 11:30 am	Church services at the Little Flat Rock
12:00 noon	Bon Voyage Luncheon

REGISTRATION FEES INCLUDE:

- 3-meat buffet at Winkerby's on Friday evening, August 9
- 3-meat catered picnic at the Root Memorial Bldg., Aug. 10
- Hot lunch on Sunday, August 11 prepared by Little Flat Rock Ladies Guild
- Each adult, age 18 and over will receive a ceramic coffee mug featuring a line drawing of the Hackleman cabin
- A donation to the Little Flat Rock Christian Church

D.A.R. NEEDS YOUR HELP: The Rushville Chapter of the D.A.R. is asking for donations of replicas--and I stress replicas--of any memorabilia they could use in the Hackleman Cabin. They are not looking for anything irreplaceable or valuable as the cabin has been broken into and vandalized twice. The cabin is rather sparse and they would like to dress it up a bit.

FAMILY RESEARCH: Indiana is rich in Hackleman family history. In 1803 Jacob[2] Hackleman (Michael[1]) came to Indiana Territory by packhorse. By 1806, all of his 14 children and their spouses had joined Jacob. From here the family grew and spread throughout Indiana and began the trek west.

Since whole families picked up and moved together, Indiana is also rich in Tyner, Perkins, Milner, Sailors, Osborn, Hawkins, Lines, Robinson, Adams, Williams, Webb, Allensworth, and Davis history.

You will want to plan enough time to visit the libraries in Rushville, Connersville and Brookville. You may also want to visit the State Archives in Indianapolis and the outstanding genealogical library at Fort Wayne.

Bring your camera. Local county maps make locating cemeteries and churches easy. We will have as many of these maps as we can, available at registration for your convenience.

DISPLAYS: Please bring your photo albums, Bibles, or any other memorabilia you would like to share.

PHOTOGRAPHER: We are making arrangements for a group photograph to be taken Saturday afternoon. This photo will be offered for sale at the lowest possible price we can manage. The photographer (my husband, M.F.A., photography) will be available Saturday afternoon if you would like other photos taken.

LODGING: A list of hotels and campgrounds is available by sending a stamped, self-addressed envelope to: Hackleman Associates, 25 Lake View Terrace, Rochester, NY 14613-1710.

RUSHVILLE IN AUGUST: The average daily temperatures range from

WHAT'S COOKING?

Friday night's buffet at Winkerby's includes roast beef, ham, fried chicken, potatoes, salad, vegetables, beverage, desert, tax and gratuity. Winkerby's is air-conditioned.

Saturday's catered picnic includes hot dogs, hamburgers, BBQ chicken, potato salad, macaroni salad, baked beans, chips, brownies, cookies, beverages, tax and gratuity. It is being catered by Winkerby's and served in the Root Building which can be closed up in the event of rain or opened up in the event of hot weather. It is located on the fairgrounds on the north side of town just a few yards from the Hackleman Cabin.

Sunday's lunch is being prepared by the Little Flat Rock Christian Church's ladies guild and includes meat, potatoes, salad, beverages, desert, tax and gratuity.

*****Winkerby's and the Little Flat Rock Christian Church reserve the right to make changes of equal value and quality if necessary.
----------◆----------
Rushville has a McDonalds, Burger King, Pizza Hut and several family style restaurants for meals not included in the registration fee.

AREA ATTRACTIONS

One of the most outstanding area attractions is **METAMORA**. Situated on the Whitewater Canal there are steam train rides, canal boat rides, and carriage rides. The shopper will find upward of a hundred small shops to chose from. There are several restaurants to chose from.

Don't miss Whitewater State Park with it's fine fishing, swimming and camping facilities. Experience walking over the same ground your ancestors did as they traveled up the Whitewater valley to settle a new territory!

Come for the "Steam Engine Festival" in Rushville. This festival is held the 1st weekend of August and includes a flea market, entertainment, log splitting contests, broom making, and a parade of steam run vehicles about every two hours. Oh yes, and an Old Calliope! Contact the Rushville Chamber of Commerce: (317) 932-2880.

Knightstown has an Antique mall, 136 W. Carey Street. Over 20,000 sq. feet of diversified stock.

On Carthage Road between Knightstown and Carthage is the Michael Bonne Copper Smith Shop with a 19th century museum workshop.

The Rushville area is home to six covered bridges.

Most of all, bring your notebooks, pencils and walking shoes so you can do "a little research" while you're here. Rushville, Connersville, Liberty, Brookville, and the surrounding area are rich in Hackleman history you won't want to miss!

REGISTRATION FORM

RESERVATIONS MUST BE <u>RECEIVED</u> BY <u>AUGUST 1, 1991</u>.

Since meal counts have to be given to the caterers, I cannot accept registrations "at the door." If for some reason you cannot return your registration form by August 1, 1991, please call (716) 458-0386 to make other arrangements.

			TOTAL
_____ Adults, age 18 and over	$53.00 each	_____
_____ Child, age 8 to age 17	$40.00 each	_____
_____ Child, age 4 to age 7	$25.00 each	_____
_____ Child, age 0 to age 3	No charge	
_____ Extra Coffee Mugs	$6.00 each	_____

TOTAL ENCLOSED _____

There is a $10.00 cancellation fee per adult, age 18 and over for cancellations received before May 1, 1991. Since there are deposits and guarantees involved there will be **No Refunds for cancellations received after May 1, 1991.

Please print:

Your name: _____

Mailing address: _____

_____

City, State, Zip: _____

Phone #: (   ) _____

Names of other persons for whom you are making reservations:

_____   _____

_____   _____

_____   _____

Please make checks or money orders payable to Hackleman Associates and mail to:

Hackleman Associates
25 Lake View Terrace
Rochester, New York 14613

THIS FORM MAY BE DUPLICATED.

Hackleman Associates
25 Lake View Terrace, Rochester, NY 14613-1710
(716) 458-0386

July 10, 1991

RE: **HACKLEMAN REUNION** August 9, 10, 11, 1991

ATTENDING: **As of July 10: 80 people from 17 states**

Dear family,

Enclosed is the final schedule of events for the union and another map in case you misplaced the one you received earlier.

FRIDAY

Your registration packages will be available at the library after 12:00 noon. Any packages not picked up there will be taken to Winkerby's restaurant Friday evening. Meal tickets will be included and will be collected by the caterers.

Please bring whatever you have to help decorate the Hackleman Cabin to be presented at the banquet Friday evening. Linda Moster of the local DAR will be present to accept donations. Again, they do not want anything valuable, just replicas, copies or photographs.

Also please bring any photos you would like to have copied. My husband, Keith, is bringing the necessary equipment to do the work there so you do not have to give up your original. He will make you an 8 x 10 black and white photo for ten dollars including postage and handling.

SATURDAY

Help is needed setting up tables and chairs at the Root Memorial Building.

There will be a meeting to form a family association beginning at noon on Saturday. In addition, the agenda will address a regular newsletter, writing a supplement to the Hackleman genealogy, and the possibility of erecting a memorial to Jacob Hackleman. Please give these matters some thought and feel free to introduce other subjects of interest.

My husband, Keith, is bringing equipment to take a group photo at the Hackleman cabin. 8 x 10 black and white prints can be ordered for ten dollars including postage and handling.

S C H E D U L E

Friday, August 9:

12 noon - 5:00 pm	Registration at the Rushville Public Library. The library opens at 9:00 am for research.
6:00 pm	Buffet dinner at Winkerby's, 205 North Main St.
7:30 pm	Presentation of items for the Hackleman Cabin
7:45 pm	Guest speaker, Jim Scott, will share his knowledge of Rush County history.

Saturday, August 10:

11:30 am	Set up tables at the Root Memorial Building
12:00 noon	Business meeting to discuss forming family association.
2:00 pm - until ?	Catered picnic at the Root Memorial Building at the Fairgrounds, about 50 yards from the Hackleman Cabin.
approx. 3:30 pm	Group photographs at the Hackleman Cabin

Sunday, August 11:

10:15 am - 11:30 am	Church services at the Little Flat Rock
12:00 noon	Bon Voyage Luncheon at the Lyons Club
1:00 pm	Guest speaker, Frances Norris, Church Historian

SUNDAY

Services begin at 10:15 am.

The Little Flat Rock Christian Church has requested we try to car pool to services on Sunday morning as their parking lot is small.

There is day care available during services.

Rev. John Sargent will be offering communion in honor of our attendance.

Directions to the Lions club are enclosed. It is approximately a half mile south of the church. The Lions Club is not air conditioned; however, I have been assured everything possible will be done to keep us cool.

Frances Norris has offered to share her knowledge of the history of the church after lunch.

GENERAL INFORMATION

Pat and Fran Clark of Texas will be bringing their camper fully equipped with a computer and a copier and have offered their use during the reunion.

County maps are no longer free; however the Rush County Chamber of Commerce has agreed to honor their promise to provide us with free maps which you will receive as part of your registration package. Other counties have a variety of fees.

DISPLAYS

There was not enough interest in sending photographs and biographies to do a display. I am returning those sent with your copy of this letter.

Burr Hackleman is creating lineage charts of all descendants attending which will be on display at the library Friday and at the Root Building on Saturday.

Sincerely,

Phyllis A. Hackleman

Phyllis A. Hackleman

FRIDAY ONLY REGISTRATION FORM

The following rates are in effect for reservations received before May 1, 1991.**

TOTAL

_____Adults, age 18 and over	$21.00 each*	_____
_____Child, age 8 to age 17	$14.50 each*	_____
_____Child, age 4 to age 7	$ 7.00 each*	_____
_____Child, age 0 to age 3	No charge	
_____Extra Coffee Mugs	$5.00 each	_____

TOTAL ENCLOSED   _____

*Add $5.00 per person for reservations received after May 1, 1991

There is a $10.00 cancellation fee per adult, age 18 and over for cancellations received before May 1, 1991. Since there are deposits and guarantees involved there will be **No Refunds for cancellations received after May 1, 1991.

Please print:

Your name:_____

Mailing address:_____

_____

City, State, Zip:_____

Phone #: (   ) _____

Names of other persons for whom you are making reservations:

_____   _____

_____   _____

_____   _____

Please make checks or money orders payable to Hackleman Associates and mail to:

Hackleman Associates
25 Lake View Terrace
Rochester, New York 14613

REGISTRATION FORM
FRIDAY NIGHT GUESTS ONLY

_____Adults, age 18 and over $00.00 each*   TOTAL
                                                         _____

Please print:

Your name: _____

Mailing Address: _____

_____

City, State, Zip: _____

Phone #:   (   ) _____

Names of other persons for whom you are making reservations:

_____

_____

_____